OTHER BOOKS BY REV. FR. KIERAN C. OKORO:

* Catechesis in the Catechumenate and Other Periods of the R.C.I.A.
* Celebrations of the R.C.I.A.
* Jesus and Non-Christian Religions

THE AMAZING GIFT
of the
PRIESTHOOD

REV. FR. KIERAN C. OKORO, PhD

FOREWORD BY BISHOP JOHN I. OKOYE

Order this book online at www.trafford.com
or email orders@trafford.com

Most Trafford titles are also available at major online book retailers.

Cover artwork by Mary Anne Trovato

Printed in the United States of America.

ISBN: 978-1-4669-3574-7 (sc)
ISBN: 978-1-4669-3573-0 (hc)
ISBN: 978-1-4669-3572-3 (e)

Library of Congress Control Number: 2012909824

Trafford rev. 06/05/2012

 www.trafford.com

North America & international
toll-free: 1 888 232 4444 (USA & Canada)
phone: 250 383 6864 ♦ fax: 812 355 4082

Contents

Foreword

The Amazing Gift of the Priesthood considers anew who the Catholic priest is in order to establish his identity. The author, Rev. Fr. Kieran C. Okoro, rightly concludes that the Catholic priesthood is a participation in the priesthood of Christ who is *the eternal* Priest. The content of the priesthood of Christ touches on the mystery of the Incarnation of the second Person of the Holy Trinity and on his expiatory sacrifice on the cross. Because of his two natures, divine and human, and his sacrifice on the cross, Christ now plays the role of Mediator between God and man. The fact that the priest, a mere man of flesh and blood, is called upon to assume the office and function of the eternal Priest, Christ, makes the ministerial priesthood an amazing gift of God, a sign of God's favor to the Church and to the unworthy recipient.

In considering the priesthood as the amazing gift, Fr. Kieran discusses some aspects of the priestly call and life that help the priest live and minister well. His discussion takes naturally to the Eucharist, which forms the center of the priest's life and ministry. He reflects on the implication of celebrating the Holy Mass. Christ is the one who offers the sacrifice of the Mass as well as the victim. He rightly devotes some thoughts to the area of human sexuality. This, for the author, is very important as improper information and formation on human sexuality could be the bane of the amazing gift of the priesthood. There is scarcely any book written on the spirituality of the priesthood that would not devote a chapter to the Blessed Virgin Mary, the Mother of Priests. The author does not miss this chapter in his book. He presents the Mother of Christ, the Mother of Priests, as the woman the priest is to love.

We all are familiar with the adage "Fear the Greek gift." Any student of ancient history would understand that it was the soldiers who were hidden in the big wooden horse left by the Greeks by the city gate of the city of Troy. Their ploy succeeded when the horse was eventually brought inside the city, even to the sacred sanctuary of the gods of the land. It was the soldiers who were hidden in the horse that eventually set ablaze the beautiful city of Troy. Using this as a metaphor, the author goes on to discuss how the enemies of the Church infiltrated into the Church and have been ordained as priests. The harm such false priests are causing to the image of the priesthood is untold. It should be noted that these enemies penetrated and are still penetrating the Church through the seminaries and other formation centers for the Catholic priesthood.

We commend the author of this work for the rich content of the exposition of the themes discussed. His use of short stories and metaphors to illustrate his theological points are quite interesting as it makes the reader get more involved. The book is timely, especially now that the image of the priesthood is blurred in many places.

This book is a *vademecum* for Catholic priests and students for the Catholic priesthood. I recommend it also to the People of God for whom, with whom, and among whom the priest exercises his priestly ministry.

+John I. Okoye
Bishop of Awgu

Introduction

"Blessed is he whom you choose and call to dwell in your courts"[1] is a common processional hymn for priests and seminarians. And it is proper. That man is indeed blessed who has been chosen to dwell in the house of God, to cherish the sweetness of the Lord, to work for God all the days of his life. One such man is the priest.

The priesthood is an amazing gift. We know that God is a pure and infinite Spirit who lives in an inaccessible light. Man, on his part, is corporeal and finite. Between him and God, therefore, there was an infinite gap, a yawning chasm. But God, out of his infinite mercy and love, wanted to bridge this unfathomable chasm for the good of the human race. He found no better way of doing this than sending into the world his Son, his eternal wisdom or word through whom he made all things. This Son of God became man and lived among men in the world.

By the Son of God thus assuming flesh, taking human nature, he bridged the gap between God and man. In his person God and man meet. By his incarnation, by the very fact of his assuming human nature, Jesus, the Son God, became the living and permanent link between God and man, the primordial connection between heaven and earth, the first bridge and the embodiment of the divine plan of redemption. He is the only name given to men by which they can be saved,[2] the only way to the Father, and no one can come to the Father except through him.[3] The essence of the priesthood belongs to him alone in his person.

His priesthood reaches its zenith at his sacrificial death on the cross. For by the paschal event, he carried his own blood into the everlasting sanctuary, winning eternal redemption for mankind.[4]

1

His priesthood lasts forever since he continues, in all times and generations, to save those who draw close to God through him.[5]

For the purpose of carrying out the Father's plan of saving the world, Jesus founded the Church, his community of salvation. This Church constitutes the historical continuation of his presence. This means the Church is the presence of Christ on earth. This becomes clear in the conversion of Saint Paul.[6] Hence, Saint Paul himself calls it the body of Christ, and the Second Vatican Council sees it in relation to Christ as a sacrament, a sign, and an instrument of salvation and of unity among men.[7] To the Church Christ gives the mandate to continue on earth until the end of time his work of giving glory to the Father and salvation to mankind. In other words, he transfers to his Church the mission given to him by his Father: "As the Father has sent me, so am I sending you."[8]

To enable it to fulfill this mission adequately, he instituted in and for the Church the sacrament of orders, which confers on some selected members of the Church the dignity and power of the priesthood. Those elevated to this dignity—bishops and priests, and in a subordinate degree, deacons—especially are to continue on behalf of Christ and his Church the priestly work of Christ, the eternal priest. In the Church, though all the baptized share in the priesthood of Christ, the priest, however, takes the place of Christ; he is the *alter Christus,* another Christ. This becomes obvious at the consecration at Mass when he, using the words of Christ, changes bread and wine into the body and blood of Christ. The priesthood is therefore an enormously exalted vocation, indeed the highest vocation, since priests take the place of Christ in the Church and the world, and without the priesthood, there is no Church. The priesthood is a great gift not only to the person who becomes a priest and the family/community from which he has been chosen, but also to the community he has been sent or works, the whole Church and the world as a whole. All should always thank God for this great gift.

Let it be known that in this book, the word *priest*, except where it is clearly stated otherwise, includes bishop and priest and, in a subordinate degree, the deacon.

Some years ago, I moderated several retreats for various groups of priests, deacons, and seminarians. Some of those who were present in those retreats had requested for the scripts of my conferences. My desire to comply with their requests has led especially to the writing of this book. I thank them for their encouragement. I am grateful also to my friend and former seminary mate, Most Rev. Dr. John I. Okoye, bishop of Awgu, who despite his tight schedule accepted to write the foreword of this book. My thanks go too to another friend of mine, Rev. Fr. Dr. Anthony Njoku of Seat of Wisdom Major Seminary, Owerri, who read through the manuscripts and offered his suggestions. I am indebted to Ludwig and Janice Geibel, Joseph and Trudy Carroll, as well as Gary and Carol Anderson, who helped me to obtain some of the books I needed for writing chapter six. I pray to God to bless them all.

✝

CHAPTER 1

The Author of the Christian Priesthood

A Short Story

Long before the arrival of Christianity in the Amala clan, Umuopara and Okorobi were two neighboring autonomous towns. Umuopara had a lot of fertile lands, sheep, and cattle, as well as skilled metal workers. It was regarded as one of the richest and most powerful towns of Amala. Its men were reputed for their bravery; no young man was counted as a man until he had been to war and proved his valor. And no man was allowed to take the title *dike* until he had brought home from war a man's head or had killed a lion. Thanks to their wealth and military power, the rulers of Umuopara had conquered some of their neighbors, killing their leaders and annexing their territory. Endowed thus with much wealth, many fertile lands, and power, Umuopara was not only respected but also even feared by many towns of Amala. Okorobi, however, was not as fortunate as its neighbor. It was poor by every human standard. With very few fertile lands and little military power, it was regarded as one of the poorest and weakest in the land. Much of the menial jobs in Umuopara were done by hired men from Okorobi. But this poor village was peace loving. Though it could not compare with Umuopara in wealth and power, it lived peacefully with the latter, and often men from both towns went on hunting trips together.

During these expeditions, they usually surrounded the piece of forest they suspected had many games. On one such expedition, Okafor of Okorobi noticed a confused movement on his right. What was it? A deer, an antelope, or what? There was no time. If he delayed more, he thought, the game would escape. He had to act immediately. And he did act. He pulled his trigger and fired in the direction of the movement. But lo! It was not an antelope. It was not a deer nor any wild animal. It was Amechi, a hunter from Umuopara! He was dead!

Consternation and unparalleled grief filled every heart of the hunting team. The wailing of the men drowned every other sound. And who would not cry when a healthy, prosperous young man dies in a hunting accident? The grief of the hunters from Umuopara soon changed into anger against their Okorobi partners, especially Okafor, who pulled the trigger. With this anger, those hunters from Umuopara wanted to kill every man from Okorobi in the hunting team. But the latter had earlier sensed the danger of lynching in reprisal and had taken to their heels before this anger could be visited on them. The two towns were thrown into turmoil and confusion. This was a hunting mistake, an uncalculated action of manslaughter. That was how the people of Okorobi saw it. Umuopara people, however, did not see it that way. They regarded the action as calculated and deliberate, aimed at their town as a challenge. They accused the men of Okorobi of killing Amechi purposely because they were envious of the wealth and progress of Umuopara. Thus the good relationship between the two towns vanished, and war seemed to be imminent.

On receiving the sad news of the hunting accident, Ezeala Njoku,[9] the traditional ruler of Okorobi, and his people lamented and even cried aloud. This was unusual. For in Amala, men as a custom did not weep in public; only women and children usually did so. But now there was the traditional ruler of an autonomous town weeping uncontrollably with almost all his subjects. That was the expression of their sorrow at the accident. In this sorrow and anguish, he and a few members of the elders, who were available then, hastily sent a delegation to Ezeala Keke, the traditional ruler of Umuopara, to express their heartfelt sorrow and sympathy. This delegation was made up of those elders and a few other men of Okorobi who were available at the time. This was another mistake. Ezeala Njoku and his men did not know that Umuopara people saw the sudden death of Amechi as automatically creating a warlike hostility between the two towns, that Okorobi was now seen as an enemy by Umuopara. This fact properly dawned on them when all the men of their delegation were seized and held as hostages. It was then that they realized their mistake. Their delegation should have been made up only of *ndi nwanwa*.

For in Amala, disputes between two communities or towns were settled only by these mediators, that is, *ndi nwanwa*[10] (meaning sons of our daughters). These were men who were natives of one town or village but whose mothers were born and raised in the other town or village. Men who were natives of Umuopara, for instance, but whose mothers were born and raised at Okorobi were regarded at Okorobi as *ndi nwanwa*. The same was true of men of Okorobi who had Umuopara as their mothers' place of origin. In either case, each of these men was seen as belonging to and interested in both communities or villages and can represent both impartially. Neither of the communities would do any harm to any of them except for very serious reasons. They were at home in either community or village. That was why they were the only effective mediators, or *ndi uko,* in serious disputes or disagreements between towns and villages in Amala clan. This was a fact that Okorobi men in their fright and sorrow forgot when they sent a hasty delegation to Umuopara.

Okorobi realized at this time that it was in a big trouble. How could it face Umuopara in war? The latter had almost everything while its new adversary had almost nothing. Now that its delegates had been seized, what was it to do next? That was what Ezeala Njoku wanted to find out from the enlarged meeting of the elders of Okorobi whom he summoned in the wake of the seizure of the delegates. Here Odueze, one of the wisest men in Okorobi, stood up, cleared his throat, and blamed Ezeala Njoku for his hasty delegation. "Ezeala Njoku," he quipped, "you are not a stranger in Amala. Every elder knows that only *ndi nwanwa* can mediate in serious disputes or disagreements between towns in this clan, and only they can go on delegation when relationships get sour. Why, then, did you act as if you did not know the custom of our people?" He sat down and was supported by several other elders. Ezeala Njoku offered his apology. The news of the hunting accident was so shocking that he could not think properly when he received it, he said. His apology was accepted by the elders who then decided to send the right delegation made up this time only of *ndi nwanwa*. It comprised five *ndi nwanwa*. Its mission was to express to the people of Umuopara the grief and sorrow of Okorobi at the hunting accident, to sue for peace, and to request the release of the members of the earlier delegation that were detained.

Umuopara received the delegation and gave the condition that must be fulfilled before peace would be made. Okorobi must hand over immediately to Umuopara the hunter who pulled the trigger that killed Amechi, or in alternative, it can hand over any other man who would be sacrificed at the town shrine in atonement to the gods of Umuopara. As soon as this condition was fulfilled, peace would be made, and the men held as hostages would be released. But should Okorobi fail to comply with this condition within eight market days, the hostages would be killed and war declared by Umuopara. The delegation came back and gave the condition to Ezeala Njoku and the elders of Okorobi.

Horror and panic could be felt even in the air at the poor village. The condition was very difficult, and Okorobi was not prepared to go to war with Umuopara. That would be its greatest mistake because it knew that it would be overrun in a matter of minutes; many of its inhabitants would be either killed or enslaved. Okorobi must therefore act quickly, or its troubles would multiply. But who would be surrendered to Umuopara? Unfortunately still, Okafor, who caused all the trouble, had died of a heart attack a few days after the death of Amechi. Whom was Okorobi to give up? The elders could not agree.

They felt guilty to forcefully hand over for death any man from their village who was not the cause of the death of Amechi. They were confused and in a stalemate. But they were aware that they had to meet the condition without much delay to avoid Umuopara's attack. Would anybody agree to die for the trouble he did not cause in order to save Okorobi? That was difficult to think of. Throughout Okorobi, an atmosphere of mourning and fear filled the air. People could be seen in small groups discussing in subdued tones the misfortune that had befallen them and trying to find consolation in one another.

Ezeala Njoku and the elders of Okorobi meanwhile spent sleepless nights trying in vain to find a way to avoid the calamity that was about to descend on their town. They had only three days more to comply with Umuopara's condition or face war. That morning, Ezeala Njoku woke up weak and moody because he did not sleep well. He washed his face and had just offered a *kola* nut to his personal god when Obioha, son of Ogudo of Okorobi, came with his uncle Ezechukwu and asked to see Ezeala Njoku. The traditional ruler's second wife, Adaku, gave them seats at the *obiriama*, a sitting room separate from the main building of the compound. Adaku informed Ezeala Njoku that these two men wanted to see him. Ezeala Njoku came out and greeted his visitors, sat down, and ordered for kola nuts. These were brought in a wooden saucer, *okwa,* by Adaku, who handed them to Ezeala Njoku and left the room. Njoku gave them to Ezechukwu, Obioha's uncle, who said a few words over them and in turn gave them to Obioha, the youngest of the three. Obioha thanked the gods and presented the kola nuts again to Ezeala Njoku, who permitted him to prepare the nuts for eating. While they were eating the nuts, Ezechukwu greeted Ezeala Njoku again and made the following short statement. "Ezeala, live forever! My nephew here, Obioha, told me something yesterday, which was beyond my comprehension. I told him to think and sleep over it and then meet me again after that. Early this morning, he called me up and repeated his statement, insisting that I accompany him to see you. That is why we are here."

After saying this, he remained silent and, with a glance and a nod, suggested to Obioha to take over.

Obioha took a deep breath, glanced around, and declared, "Ezeala, live forever! I am the first son of Ogudo. The misfortune that has befallen our town has been very disturbing to every one of us. Probably I would not be exaggerating if I say that my own anguish is more than that of most other men in Okorobi. Why? Because I love my town very much and would not like it to be destroyed by Umuopara. I know if Okorobi is attacked, my family and I are not in great danger for my brothers and I are *ndi nwanwa* at Umuopara." Ezeala Njoku was becoming impatient. With the great danger dangling over his town, he had no time to listen to long speeches. He raised his hand and ordered the young man to make his point quickly. Obioha nodded and continued. "Yes, my mother was born and raised at Umuopara. Well, I repeat that I do not wish any harm to fall on Okorobi, my beloved town. We have only two days more to meet the ultimatum given by Umuopara. Has our town found a solution to the demand? Has anybody been found yet to be given to Umuopara?" He paused, expecting an answer. Ezeala Njoku shook his head, which was the same as saying no, wondering what Obioha was in his home for. Obioha glanced at the face of Njoku again, took another deep breath, and continued. "Ezeala, I wish to offer a solution." Njoku seemed to be jolted and now fixed his eyes on him, wondering what the solution would be. Young Obioha continued. "I wish to offer myself to be given to Umuopara so that Okorobi may be saved, to die so that our town and its inhabitants may not be destroyed."

Ezeala Njoku was stunned at this statement. Though he desired to find a solution to the problem that faced him and his town, he could not understand how anyone in his senses would volunteer to die for the town when he was not even one of those in the hunting expedition that claimed the life of Amechi and caused the whole problem. Njoku could not believe Obioha was serious. He thanked the young man and his uncle and invited them to come again in the evening. Immediately Ezeala Njoku sent for Akajiafo, his closest adviser. On his arrival, after briefing him of the latest developments, Njoku ordered him to sound the second wooden gong at about noon. This gong was usually sounded when the traditional ruler wanted to summon the elders of the town in emergency. Town criers also were sent for the same purpose to the remote parts of the locality where the sound of the gong was either faint or not heard at all. Diala and Chukwuma were in the latter's hut, discussing the problem that had befallen their town, when they heard the gong. They guessed that this summons was not unconnected with the same problem. Since these two men were free that time, they set out walking to Ezeala Njoku's house. They were among the earliest arrivals to the summons. By early evening, many of the elders had taken their seats.

Seated also were Obioha and his uncle. Almost all the elders were surprised to see in their midst Obioha, who was only in his twenties. What could have brought him here? they wondered. Did he come to represent anybody—even though it is not usual in their clan for an elder to be represented by a young man in a serious discussion such as the elders of Okorobi have now? Or was he running some errand? They could have asked themselves a hundred similar questions but could not have found the exact answer. When almost all the elders had assembled, Ezeala Njoku came out with kola nuts. (Kola nuts were customarily presented to visitors and friends on their arrival at the host's home. It was a sign of welcome or acceptance. In Amala, no serious discussion was ever begun until the nuts had been presented, shared, and eaten.) Ezeala Njoku presented the nuts to Akajiafo, who in turn gave them to Mbonu, the oldest of the elders. And since there were many of these elders, Mbonu decided that it was better the kola nuts were passed only to the kindred heads instead of to individuals for their acceptance. For, as a custom, the nuts had also to be passed round the group before they were broken and eaten. As they were eating the nuts, Ezeala Njoku greeted the elders and made a brief statement. "We all know the problem that faces our dear town at this time," he began. "Everyone here knows the efforts we have made to no avail to meet Umuopara's almost impossible condition. We have now barely two days to comply with this condition or face war. Last night I could not sleep. My mind roamed far and wide, wondering all night what would become of this town if Umuopara were to invade it. Early this morning, while these thoughts were still going through my heated head, this young man, *Obioha*, came to me with his uncle and said something which I think is better said before you. Now, my son, *Obioha*, repeat before the elders of Okorobi what you said to me." He sat down. Obioha stood up, greeted the elders, and repeated before them that he was ready to volunteer his life to save Okorobi from Umuopara's invasion.

On hearing this, the elders could not restrain their emotions. For sheer joy, in fact, many of them behaved like mere children. Some of them danced around; others came and carried Obioha high, chanting improvised songs of praise for him. Soon the news spread through the town. The fear and grief in many hearts were lifted, especially the hearts of cowards and children. At last someone has been found, or rather someone has volunteered to die so that Okorobi might be saved. Yet there were mixed feelings among many of the people. Obioha was a good and very promising young man who had, for several times, led his town's wrestling team to victory in the wrestling competitions of Amala. He loved his town so much that he would do anything he could for its welfare. He was a patriot who had the qualities of a good leader. His patriotism could be shown by the fact that he was going to die to forestall a conflict he was not the cause. Some people's emotions moved from happiness and joy to sorrow and pity for an innocent man who was going to sacrifice his life for his town. They wished they could avoid this death. But since Umuopara left no other options, Okorobi had to accept the offer voluntarily made by Obioha.

Meanwhile, Umuopara was waiting impatiently for a response or rather fulfillment of its demands. Its men were preparing for war right from the day they gave their difficult condition to Okorobi, convinced that the latter would not be able to meet that condition within the limited time. They thought that was a good opportunity for them to annex that town to their own. So three days before the final date, the elders and commanders of their warriors assembled at the compound of Ezeala Keke. Many of them were already rejoicing at the prospect of invading Okorobi. It would be a chance for them to loot and make themselves rich at the expense of the enemy. Their first target would be Ezeala Njoku's compound. He and other elders were to be captured alive, brought to the palace of Ezeala Keke to be mocked and tortured before they would be killed at the town shrine to avenge the death of Amechi and appease their gods. After the capture of these important men, Umuopara's warriors would have the freedom to loot to their satisfaction and to kill anybody they wished, only they would be instructed not to harm women and children. These would be taken to Umuopara to serve as maids and servants. These promises made the invasion even more attractive to greedy men.

They were, however, disappointed when, a day before the deadline, Okorobi responded. It sent Obioha, accompanied by nineteen other *ndi nwanwa* to Umuopara. These arrived at the home of Ezeala Keke. After the usual protocols of sharing *kola* nuts, the leader of the delegation, Obika, made a short speech to the effect that he and his group had come as a delegation from Okorobi to satisfy Umuopara's demand; they had come with a man to be handed over. Having said this, he went to Obioha's seat, took him by the hand, and handed him to Ezeala Keke in the presence of some elders of Umuopara who were with him when the delegation arrived. The traditional head took a deep breath, heaved out a sigh, and remained silent for a moment and then made his comment. He accepted the ransom and thanked the gods who had helped to prevent the invasion that was imminent.

That afternoon, the medium wooden gong at the compound of Ezeala Keke sounded intermittently, indicating a summons of the elders of Umuopara. Some, on hearing the gong, thought it was a summons to a last consultation before the invasion of Okorobi. When the elders came, however, after the usual sharing of kola nuts, Ezeala Keke presented Obioha to them. He made known to them that the ransom had been brought to him by Okorobi in fulfillment of Umuopara's demand. Many roared, praising their traditional head and their town. Some others regretted the fact that Okorobi fulfilled their demand on time, thereby denying them the chance of looting and of showing off their valor. The elders handed to Okorobi's delegation the members of the earlier delegation who were held as hostages by Umuopara. The delegation left for Okorobi, leaving Obioha behind at Umuopara. There and then, the day was fixed for sacrificing Obioha to the gods of Umuopara. It would be in the midmorning on *Eke* market day. Meanwhile, Ogadi, the special assistant to the traditional head, was to keep Obioha in his custody until the fixed day.

Ogadi took Obioha without chains or shackles to his home. The prisoner moved freely in the compound but was forbidden to leave Ogadi's homestead at any time. Even at night, he was left free in the room assigned to him. From the first day this young prisoner arrived at Ogadi's home, the special assistant's youngest wife, Ugomma, who was about two years younger than Obioha, conceived much love for him. Cashing in on her husband's love for her, she persistently pleaded for forgiveness for Okorobi and the release of Obioha. Her husband made it clear to her that he could do little since the matter was not in his hands alone but was the concern of the whole town. Even though Obioha received enough food, Ugomma secretly provided him with some delicacies such as fruits, sweetened meat, and fish. And when she realized that her plea for the prisoner's release was useless, she decided to help Obioha to escape. She was not only surprised but also rather shocked when Obioha refused her offer and told her that he had freely volunteered to die for his people.

The day of the sacrifice came. Almost all in Umuopara turned out for the spectacle, which would take place in the town market square. People assembled according to their ages, ranks in society, and sexes, the elders having their seats in front, close to Ezeala Keke. The market square was filled almost beyond its capacity, and people were treading on one another. Then Ogadi, the special assistant, led a group of young men who brought in Obioha, now in chains. Ogadi raised his right hand in gesticulation of power and bellowed in the air, "Umuopara *kwenu!*" The people responded *"Ho-oh!"* He turned on the right and bellowed again *"Kwenu!"* He received another round of *"Ho-oh!"* When he turned on the left and made the same cry, he received a similar cheer. Then all was quiet. Ogadi, with Obioha in chains, went to Ezeala Keke and handed him back to the traditional head. Many in the crowd strove to catch a glimpse of the man who was going to die in less than an hour and a half from then. Ezeala Keke stood up to address his people. He briefly narrated the circumstances that brought about the gathering and the necessity of the sacrifice to the gods. He tried to exonerate his town from the death of Obioha, which he said was demanded by the gods as expiation for the blood of Amechi that was shed by Okorobi men. As he presented Obioha again to the people, many roared and cheered the traditional head. Some women were very sympathetic; among them was Ugomma, who was weeping. Others did not care. Like the Roman mob, they enjoyed seeing other people suffer and die. Many of such people laughed and made fun of the whole affair. When he had finished his speech, the traditional head handed Obioha to Ugorji, the chief priest of *Ala*, the land goddess. Ugorji then led the prospective victim to the shrine, which was in the same square, to present him to the gods and then give the deathblow. The blood was to be poured around the shrine, and the body would be burned around its precincts.

Now the zero hour had come. It was clear to everybody that Obioha was going to die in a matter of minutes. The chief priest presented him to the gods with a short prayer, pleading that the gods accept the sacrifice and be appeased. He was almost ready to give the deathblow. He had already smeared his eyebrows with the traditional mixture of ground roots, alligator pepper, and chalk, which made him look awesome or rather fearsome. As for Obioha, though he had volunteered to suffer for his people, the thought of dying a tragic death in public now became repulsive. Fear gripped him, and some regretful thoughts tried to jump into his heart. But he pushed these out by reminding himself that it was necessary that he die so that his town might be saved. Yet, despite his resolution to sacrifice himself, the realization that he would die soon made his anguish so gnawing that big drops of sweat streamed down from his whole body. A few minutes now, he would be blindfolded and struck dead! Just before then, he asked for permission to make his last statement before the crowd. When this permission was given, he made the following statement, which looks like a hymn:

> Ezeala Keke, live forever. Umuopara live forever.
> My dear people of Umuopara, I love you, I love you;
> Okorobi, my town, I love too; I love Okorobi too.
> The death of Amechi was indeed a great tragedy;
> That tragedy has brought you and me here,
> Not that I was the cause of his death or any evil.
>
> No, it is because of my love, love for Okorobi dear,
> And love for its sister, Umuopara, my maternal home.
> Yes, you know me sure; I am nwanwa of Umuopara.
>
> It does no good for two sister towns to shed blood,
> The blood of many of their citizens in war unneeded.
> That is why I have come to die, to save many others.
>
> But nobody has forced me or paid so that I may die;
> I freely chose to die to save my brothers and sisters.
> I sincerely request that my death may bring peace.

Though this speech was improvised and lacked oratorical skill, all present listened to it attentively. By the time Obioha finished talking, many of the women and children in the crowd were in tears. Here was an innocent man, they reasoned, who surrendered his life so that others might live. They could not take it in. Most of the men, on the other hand, argued that since he gave himself up voluntarily, he had to die to placate the gods.

The chief priest who was to give the deathblow was ready. He came forward with his sword. But as he stepped toward Obioha, a thought seemed to flash through his head. He stopped, went back into the shrine, and within a few minutes, sent for Ezeala Keke, some other leading elders, and other high-ranking priests of *Ala*. He told them that before he was about to give the deathblow, something seemed to tell him to consult the gods again before Obioha's death. He made the consultation and found out that the gods would not accept the death of Obioha. Why? Because, first of all, he was *nwanwa* of Umuopara, and secondly, he was innocent. Therefore, he would not die. But because he loved Umuopara so much that he was ready to give his life to appease the gods, his voluntary surrender of his life is an interior sacrifice acceptable to the gods; that sacrifice was accepted by the gods as sufficient. Therefore, there was no need for his physical death.

Meanwhile, the pain of waiting for so long for the deathblow became more agonizing than death itself for young Obioha, who was already tied to the stakes. Those few minutes became like hours as he wondered what was delaying his dispatch to the land of the dead. At last, Ezeala Keke emerged from the shrine, and all eyes were fixed on him. He called for silence and then addressed the crowd again. He told them that it was not the wish of the gods that Obioha should die because of the two reasons given above. Many in the crowd shouted in joy and interrupted him with a long applause. There were tears of joy in many eyes. But others who wanted to feast their eyes by watching a human being murdered in public were disappointed. Ezeala Keke continued, "The gods also accept his interior sacrifice as enough. His surrendering of himself for death suffices to appease the gods. So he will go free. On my part, I am very much pleased with Obioha. He is a great and generous man, a hero. In consultation with the elders who went into the shrine with me, in appreciation of what he has done, I hereby confer on him the title of *Omeudo I of Umuopara*. In addition, since he is *nwanwa* of Umuopara and a special one, we shall build him a house at Umuopara. He is free to live here and have all the rights and privileges of the citizens of Umuopara. But whether he chooses to live at Umuopara or Okorobi, from now forward, he will be consulted in any of our dealings with Okorobi, and his advice will be taken very seriously. This privilege is for him and his descendants in perpetuity. So his second title is therefore *Special Nwanwa I of Umuopara.*" This means mediator of mediators in relations with Okorobi.

In the afternoon of that same day, Obioha came back to Okorobi to tell the story of his ordeal or rather adventure. He first went to his home to see his family. His uncle and other members of the family, who were in anguish over his presumed death, thinking they saw a ghost when he came, shouted and ran away. But he called out and assured them that he was alive. As would be expected, their joy knew no bounds when they became sure that he was actually alive. After a brief stay with his family, he went with his uncle again to see the traditional head of Okorobi. Ezeala Njoku was stunned again. He gave a loud shout and started dancing round his compound. His wives and their daughters were watching from their huts. They wondered what had happened to the traditional head. Was he drunk, or had he suddenly become crazy? He was none of these. But he was full of joy and surprise. He danced for about four minutes and came back to his seat. Since it was already late, he could not summon his people to break the good news to them. He only sent for his special adviser with whom he first shared the news. That night, joy and wild thoughts did not allow him to sleep soundly. What were he and his town to do for Obioha to repay him in appreciation for his voluntary surrender of his life to save Okorobi? What gift would be sufficient? There was no title too great to confer on him. These were among the questions and thoughts that were roaming in Ezeala Njoku's head that night.

In the morning, he summoned the elders to share the news with them and deliberate on what would be the best reward for Obioha. Just like Ezeala Njoku himself, many of the elders were beside themselves with joy. There and then, the title of *agunechembal* (or chief guardian) of Okorobi was conferred on Obioha. It was further decided that he would take over as special adviser, succeeding Akajiafo, who was retiring because of age. In addition, he would succeed Ezeala Njoku as traditional head of the town when the latter, who had no male issue, would die. For it was already their custom that if a traditional head was not survived by a male issue, his place would be passed to a worthy son of the land determined by the elders and the gods. Even though no member of his family had been traditional head or had a right to the headship of Okorobi, Obioha was made the prospective heir of the leadership of his town. Later, the generality of the town was summoned and told about the outcome of Obioha's adventure.

The First Time Things Fell Apart

I hope the foregoing short story can throw a little light into the understanding of the fracture of the original harmony between God and his creation and the mending or repairing of that fracture. Man, by his sin of disobedience, threw into disarray the harmony that the Creator had established. This was the first time that things fell apart. By severing his good relationship with God, he became afraid and realized that he was naked. This nakedness was not necessarily physical nakedness. Rather, after his sin, when he had cut himself from God's protection, he realized how defenseless and insecure he was.

Something had to be done to restore that good relationship, to build a bridge and reestablish harmony, to reconcile God and man and make the latter pleasing and acceptable to God.

Let us now use some points of the story above to consider Christ's sacrifice and mediation. First of all, Obioha had much love for his people and therefore freely offered himself in their place, to die so that they might live. Even when he became sure he was going to die, he did not recant his free self-offering, not because he loved death, but because he was rather convinced his death would help to avert war between the two communities and hence save many from dying. Furthermore, he was a native of Okorobi and *nwanwa* of Umuopara and thereby qualified as a natural mediator between the two communities.

Jesus' love for the human race is even greater, which made him humble himself to take the nature of a creature. He accepted his death freely as something necessary in his mission; for him it was a sacrificial death for the redemption of the world. And he is more qualified right from the moment of his birth to be the natural mediator between God and the human race. For he is God from all eternity, of the same substance with God the Father and equal with him. But owing to his love for us human beings, he came down from heaven and became man born of the Virgin Mary through the power of the Holy Spirit.[11] Thus, thanks to his two natures, divine and human, God and man meet in him. This means that by his incarnation, by the very fact of his assuming human nature, the Son of God bridged the unfathomable chasm between God and the human race and thus became necessarily the natural mediator between God and humans. "Christ, the Redeemer of the world, is the one Mediator between God and men and there is no other name under heaven by which we can be saved."[12] His priesthood, therefore, is not incidental or accidental. It is rather "integral to his identity as the Son Incarnate, as God-made-man."[13] And by voluntarily sacrificing himself on the Cross, he brought the highest priestly act to perfection. By his sacrificial death on Calvary (together with his resurrection), he reopened the way of communication between God and the human race, which was closed by sin. With his mystery and mission as priest, which, as stated above, started immediately he became man and reached their completion in his sacrifice on the cross. In Christ God seeks man and finds him. Man also makes a response of faith. "It is a response in which man speaks to God as his Creator and Father, a response made possible by that one Man who is also the consubstantial Word in whom God speaks to each individual person and by whom each individual person is enabled to respond to God."[14] And by the paschal event, he carried his own blood and entered into the eternal sanctuary, winning eternal redemption for the human race.[15] Hence, relationship between God and man passes through him. He is the one mediator between God and the human race (1 Tim. 2:5). Jesus has exercised his priesthood fully from the moment he took his seat as high priest at the right hand of God the Father in heaven, interceding for his people.[16]

Thenceforward, there is only one priesthood, the priesthood of Christ, of which the priesthood of the Old Covenant was a "prefigurement and a preparation."[17] Jesus represents both God reaching out to mankind and mankind responding to God's offer. He is the living personification of the dialogue of salvation and the embodiment of the divine plan of redemption. Thus, the essence of the priesthood belongs to Jesus alone in his very person. He is the primordial link between God and man, the first bridge and first bridge builder between heaven and earth. And he rightly claims to be that ladder reaching from heaven to earth through which heaven and earth communicate,[18] the only way to the Father, and no one can reach the Father except through him.[19] All our prayers go to the Father through him; hence, the Church usually prays or concludes its prayers with "through Jesus Christ our Lord." His priesthood has no end since he lives forever, continually saving all those who draw near to God through him.[20]

The Sacrifice of Christ

It should be of interest to all Christians, especially priests, to know how Christ's death is a sacrifice or rather what gives his death sacrificial and saving value. Let us continue to use our story to illustrate this.

We noted in the foregoing story that though Obioha eventually did not die a physical death as envisaged, his unflinching self-donation for the love of his people was seen and accepted by *Ala*, the goddess of Umuopara, as a complete sacrifice, which was sufficient to placate that goddess. Despite the fact that he had neither heard the Christian message nor known the Bible, his sacrifice completely conformed to the ideal sacrifice as demanded by the Holy Book. For in various passages, the Bible points out that the value of the external rite depends on the interior disposition.[21] The temptation that has always faced worshippers has been to attach much importance to the external rite and neglect the interior disposition. Some have misunderstood the prophets' warning against this as a condemnation of sacrifices. Prophets do not condemn sacrifices but rather the counterfeit of sacrifices. Why? Because without proper interior disposition, the disposition of the heart, the external rite is reduced to empty hypocrisy, which is displeasing to God.[22] Proper internal disposition is the very essence of sacrifice and not the accessory of the rite.[23] Sometimes it takes the place of the rite.[24] And the Bible presents a living synthesis of internal sacrifice, one incarnate in a person. The Servant of God of Deutero-Isaiah, especially Isaiah 53, offers his life as sacrifice for the ransom of many. The Servant freely substitutes himself for sinners. His sacrifice rooted in total obedience to God and hence, without defect, becomes beneficial for "many" according to God's plan. Here one finds the deepest interior disposition united with the greatest possible sacrifice or gift, and hence one that has great value.[25]

The New Testament identifies the Servant of God as Jesus of Nazareth, whose passion was prophesied by Deutero-Isaiah. A few instances will justify this statement. In Luke 22:37, Jesus quotes Isaiah 53:12 in relation to himself. "I tell you these words of Scripture have to be fulfilled in me; 'He let himself be taken for a criminal.' Yes what Scripture says about me is now reaching its fulfillment." In Acts 3:13, 26; 4:27, 30; and especially Acts 8:26ff, the account of the conversion of the Ethiopian eunuch, Jesus is clearly identified as the Servant of the Lord of Deutero-Isaiah. So also do 1 Peter 2:22-25 and many other passages of the New Testament. Thus, the New Testament makes it clear that Jesus was not offered up but that he chose freely to lay down his life. As he himself says, "I lay down my life in order to take it up again. No one takes it from me, but I lay it down on my own. I have power to lay it down and power to take it up again."[26] His action revealed and put into effect God's will or action. He had assumed unconditionally in his own will God's eternal plan of salvation. Jesus knew that the fate of fallen man could only be reversed by his carrying out this divine plan of salvation and that he was the only person who could bring that about, the only one who could take the scroll and to open it.[27] His whole life was one of total obedience to the will of the Father. It reached its highest point at his

THE AMAZING GIFT of the PRIESTHOOD

death.[28] It was through this total obedience that he brought about the salvation of the world. For since, through his disobedience, man brought death and ruin on himself, through total obedience, the Son of God had to bring back life to man and make him righteous before God.[29] Jesus' obedience, even unto death, is an act of religion and love by which the human race in the person of its head returns to the Father and finds life and friendship with God once more. The obedience of Jesus and his love are reversible—that is, his obedience is his love and vice versa. It was his love both for the Father and for us that made him humble himself to death, even death on the cross.[30] His love for the world is rooted in the eternal love of the Father. In other words, it is a revelation of God's love for the world.[31] We believe that Jesus, as God, is of one substance with God the Father and equal with him. Yet as man, he was totally obedient to the Father's will. His death was a resumé or summary of his life of total obedience to the Father. He was obedient to the Father's plan or will onto death in order to save the disobedient human race. His sacrifice on Calvary was first and foremost an interior sacrifice. It was primarily a sacrifice of obedience to the Father's will, that will that must be done, not Jesus' human will.[32]

Here it should not be thought, however, that Christ's sacrificial death was necessary to placate God the Father. That issue was a nagging problem among the patristics and scholars of the medieval period up to Saint Anselm. We do not intend to go into that issue here. Suffice it here to bear in mind that man's salvation was brought about by God. This needs to be explained a little

Let it be clear from the outset that God the Father took no pleasure in the death of Jesus. He is not a wicked or callous God who must be appeased by the excruciating and most humiliating death of his Son. To hold that idea is to fall back into mythology. When expressions giving such an idea are found in the Church's teaching or documents, the reader should endeavor to extract the true meaning. Christ's death was not to placate the Father but rather to bring back man, who had erred or strayed away from God.

A story from a family mishap may be used here to poorly illustrate this. A noble man of a certain village had two sons whom he loved dearly. The younger son, through his carelessness and stubbornness, fell into a deep ditch in the forest where ravines and landslides were common. When the family got to know of this, the father gathered as many people as he could to help the young man come out. The ditch was so deep that no ladder was long enough even to reach half the depth. A very long rope was thrown down, and instructions were yelled to the fallen son to seize the rope so that he would be pulled out. But he was too weak to grasp this lifeline, owing to the injuries he sustained during the accident and due to the fact that he had been without food or drink for many hours. It would need a strong man to go into the ditch and literally carry the young man out. The father was in a state of both desperation and hope. In desperation, in that if the young man was not out of the ditch in a short time, he would die and be lost to the family forever. At the same time, he had some hope that since the victim was still alive, there might be some possibility of his rescue, even though he was not sure of the means of actualizing this possibility. In this rather confused state of mind, the father promised very attractive rewards to any man who would succeed in taking his son out of the ditch. Many men would have been willing to undertake the adventure and win the rewards. But owing to the extreme risk it involved and the rare chance of success, none actually came forward for it.

As the day wore on, the hope of finding a capable and willing person either within or outside the village waned. Then the father and his remaining son had a sudden discussion on the matter. Both father and son saw the mishap as a family problem or challenge. Were they to abandon the younger son in his agonizing, slow death? If not, what else were they to do next? These and similar questions they posed to themselves. It was the son who considered himself the only man in the neighborhood who was capable of undertaking the task of rescuing his brother. He therefore volunteered to go down into the ditch in order to accomplish this. He would be let down by a long rope and would be pulled out carrying his brother on his shoulder. The father accepted this offer not because he did not love his older son, but rather because that was the only way of rescuing the younger son.

This is only a poor illustration from a human family mishap. God the Father should be praised and thanked for offering his only son to rescue fallen man. He so loved the world that he gave his only Son for the salvation of the world. In the case of the young man considered above, both sons were natural sons of the noble man. But in the case of the salvation of man—that is, the human race—we are not natural sons of God but only adopted sons or children. Yet the Father condescended to give us his Son to rescue or save us who, through our own disobedience, put ourselves in a position we could not in any way save ourselves. Praise also belongs to the Son who, though was in the form of God, did not consider equality with God a thing to be grasped. He rather humbled himself and became obedient unto death on the cross. This was why God gave him a name that is above every other name.[33]

Redemption proceeds from God the Father. For it was God's saving will that established the life of Jesus, which reaches its fulfillment in death. This death, in turn, makes God's saving will manifest and irrevocable. In other words, Jesus' death revealed how much God loves the world. Bringing back fallen man to God or conversion of man was brought about through God's redemptive will and action, which render man capable of entering into dialogue with God once more. God revealed in Jesus' saving death both his love and righteousness or justice. In the death of his Son, he made these actual, palpable, and present. Through Jesus' obedience, God renewed his invitation to the human race to enter into saving dialogue with him.

This surrender to the Father's will is the core of the sacrifice of Christ. It is this interior sacrifice that gives the external or physical death its saving and sacrificial value or meaning. Without it, his death would not have brought salvation at all. Therefore, in discussing man's salvation, it is important to note that the decisive thing, the thing in Jesus' death that brought about this salvation, was not simply the degree of his suffering; it was especially his inner disposition, the disposition to remain obedient even through all the pain and humiliation.[34] It was this inner disposition that actually made his death on the cross a sacrifice.[35]

Jesus himself intended his death to be a sacrifice. He himself announces his suffering and death by using exactly the terms that characterize the vicarious sacrifice of the Servant of God: he came to "serve" and to "give his life" "as a ransom" for "many."[36] Furthermore, the paschal context of the Last Supper[37] constitutes an intentional, precise connection between the death of Jesus and the sacrifice of the paschal lamb. In addition, Jesus goes back to Exodus 24:8 by using the formula of Moses (at the covenant of Sinai), "blood of the covenant."[38] This triple reference to the paschal lamb, whose blood delivers the Hebrews, to the victims of Sinai, whose blood seals the Old Covenant, to the Servant of God, whose expiatory and vicarious death becomes a ransom for many, clearly shows the sacrificial character of the death of Jesus. His death (and resurrection) brings about the remission of sins for many, the making of the new and everlasting Covenant, the birth of the new People of God, and assurance of redemption. These effects stress the saving role of the sacrifice of Calvary; death becomes the means of life. Jesus, in John 17:19, summarizes the effect of his death in these words: "I consecrate myself for them, so that they also may be consecrated in truth." The Eucharist, the reenactment, in the context of a banquet, of the unique sacrifice of Calvary, relates the new rite of Christians to the ancient communion sacrifices.[39] Thus, Jesus' sacrifice on the cross (and its sacramental reenactment in the Eucharist) recapitulates the sacrifices of the Old Testament. It is at once a holocaust, an expiatory offering, a communion sacrifice, as well as the making (or renewal) of the covenant. Though there is a continuation between the two Testaments, the sacrifice of Jesus far surpasses the varied and multiple sacrifices of the Old Testament by its uniqueness being the sacrificial death of God's Son and by its universal efficacy; through it the human race was redeemed.[40] In a word, the salvation of the world comes through the priestly ministry of the Son of God, Jesus Christ, who by his paschal mystery became the first priest of the new covenant and the author of both our religion and our priesthood.

✝

CHAPTER 2

The Amazing Gift

The Identity and Dignity of the Priest

It was a summer day in 2006. The village of Umuoha was agog, adorned with festive wreaths and festoons on major roads. Jubilation could be felt in the air. What was happening? Was the governor or president visiting this remote village? No, for the people, something more important than the passing visit of a great political figure or national celebrity was going to happen. They were going to receive a special blessing once more. Their own son Barnabas was going to be ordained a priest that day, the third priest from this small village in three years. On that bright day, a joyous mammoth crowd gathered at Holy Angels Cathedral; it was filled to its capacity even before the ordination ceremony began. There were eighteen candidates for ordination. Everybody was anxious to see what was happening around the sanctuary. The ceremony, which started at 9:00 a.m., ended at 1:15 p.m. At the very moment of ordination (that is, at the consecration or ordination prayer after the imposition of hands), there were cannon fires of joy and thanksgiving to God for the gift of eighteen new priests to the diocese. Kneeling before the bishop for the anointing of his hands, Father Barnabas heard the choir sing,

"*You are a priest forever, a priest like Melchizedek of old.*" His heart was filled with joy that was otherworldly, such joy that seemed to come directly from heaven. There and then he prayed to God to help him to be a holy priest. Still standing in the sanctuary, he prayed to Mary, the mother of Jesus, to help him keep all the vows he had taken. After the ordination, the ordaining bishop, who was also the ordinary of the diocese, asked for the new priests' blessing. Almost embarrassed and flattered to be the one chosen to say the prayer of blessing over his ordinary, Father Barnabas extended his hands over the bowed head of the bishop and blessed him with what words he could improvise. He and his brother, newly ordained priests, also blessed other priests present and then the whole congregation. Together with their bishop and other priests and with hearts full of joy and thanksgiving, the new priests processed out, singing with the congregation, "*Priestly people, kingly people, holy people, God's chosen people, sing praise to the Lord.*" Despite the fact that the new priests blessed the whole congregation inside the cathedral, as they stepped out, many people surged to be touched or blessed individually by each of the new priests. The priests seemed willing to bless all who came, but Father Barnabas was soon restrained by older priests who took charge of him, knowing by common sense and experience that it was impossible for him to give his blessing to all who came for it that day.

On his way home, Father Barnabas could see that the road was decorated from the parish church to his father's house and that almost all his people turned out to give him a hero's welcome. As the car conveying him moved slowly to his home, he saw men and women as old as his father and mother, others of his own age, and others younger or older all lined up along the street to give him a kingly welcome. He was strongly touched by this gesture of honor and joy. When the people caught sight of the car conveying him passing slowly, they waved enthusiastically. About a mile to his father's house, he alighted from his car to walk along with his numerous admirers. With them, he danced home to the sound of cultural dances. But before he could walk about a block, four men of his own age grade came and lifted him high, carrying him on their shoulders until they reached his father's house. Just before those carrying him could step into the compound, twenty-one cannon shots were fired for his triumphal return. Here, feasting and dancing continued until late at night, when they repaired to their homes to prepare for the following day.

The following day, Sunday, was the day of the first Mass of the new priest. Concelebrating with him was a great number of Priests, including his former teachers (or rather formators) in the seminary. After the Mass, there were many more blessings, first of his parish priest, other priests, his parents and family members, and then the whole congregation. A very grand reception followed. He received a lot of gifts and a lot of praise for his perseverance. Thanks to the solemnity of the occasions of Fr. Barnabas's ordination and first Mass, the rejoicing at these occasions, and all the honor done to this new priest by his people, four young men in his village were inspired to desire becoming priests. They are now studying in the seminary.

One of the priests in the long and slow motorcade of Father Barnabas from the cathedral to his home was Father Paul. Riding with him in his car was a seminarian, Daniel, whose vacation spiritual director Father Paul was. As the car moved slowly along, Daniel asked Father Paul a good number of questions about the priesthood and related issues. Father Paul answered the questions in great detail.

Daniel: Father, I do not understand properly what the Second Vatican Council means by the common priesthood of the faithful. What is the real distinction between it and the ministerial priesthood?

Fr. Paul: What the council means is that the Church of Christ is made up of a priestly people. Jesus founded it, and intends it to spread to every part of the world. Of this Church, he is the head and it is his mystical body. The members of the Church or the Christian faithful constitute the People of God, that is, the people who have become members of God's family thanks to Jesus' redeeming sacrifice and covenant on the cross. This people shares in the triple office and mission of Jesus Christ: the office and mission of Priest, Prophet, and King. For Christ, the primordial high priest made the new people a kingdom of priests to God, his Father (cf. Rev. 1:6). Christians join this people through the sacraments of initiation by which they are consecrated as a holy priesthood for God.[41] And through their daily works, they can offer spiritual sacrifices to God and proclaim his perfection and marvelous deeds. This is the common priesthood of the faithful. In other words, the lay faithful ordinarily participate in Christ's priestly office by offering their daily activities or rather their daily lives to God and by participating at the Eucharistic celebration or the Mass. "For all their works, prayers, and apostolic undertakings, family and married life, daily work, relaxation of mind and body, if they are accomplished in the Spirit—indeed even the hardships of life if patiently . . . borne—all these become spiritual sacrifices acceptable to God through Jesus Christ. In the celebration of the Eucharist these may most fittingly be offered to the Father along with the body of the Lord."[42] To put it in other words, "the faithful, by virtue of their royal priesthood, participate in the offering of the Eucharist. They exercise that priesthood, too, by the reception of the sacraments, by prayer and thanksgiving, the witness of a holy life, abnegation and active charity."[43]

But apart from this common priesthood, there is also the ministerial or hierarchical priesthood, that is, the priesthood of the men who have received the sacrament of orders, ordained priests just like Fr. Barnabas. The priest is the one who "makes Christ, the Savior of all men, sacramentally present to his brothers and sisters, in both their personal and social lives." And it is the presence and ministry of priests in the Church that guarantee the first proclamation of the Gospel, the ceaseless renewal of the Church, and above all, the full certainty of its fidelity and its visible continuity.[44] Though the ministerial priesthood and the priesthood of the faithful share in the one priesthood of Christ, they differ not only in degree, but also in essence and are ordered one to another.[45]

In Jesus, the whole Church is united to the Father through the Holy Spirit for the salvation of the human race. Let alone, the Church cannot accomplish this task. Its entire mission by its nature requires communion with its Lord, Jesus Christ. Thanks to this indissoluble union with its head, the Church ceaselessly receives from him all that it needs to lead men to God. In this vital union lies the basis for the ministerial priesthood. For through this ministry, the ministry of his priests who take his place as head, Jesus continues to accomplish in his Church "the work which, as Head of his Body, belongs to him alone." Thus, the ministry of priests renders the actual work of Christ palpable and "gives witness to the fact that Christ has not separated Himself from the Church."[46] For "in the midst of the community which, in spite of its defects, lives by the Spirit," the priest is "a pledge of the salvific presence of Christ."[47] In other words, "the specificity of the ministerial priesthood lies in the need that the faithful have of the mediation and the dominion of Christ, which is made visible by the work of the ministerial priesthood."[48] This is why the Church considers the ministerial priesthood a great gift given to it by Jesus Christ to continue his own saving work on earth till the end of time.

It is through ordination that "a specific ontological bond which unites the priest to Christ, High Priest and Good Shepherd" is forged. This means that the priest is, in a special way, configured into the image of Christ in the Church. Therefore, the identity of the priest has to be sought not in worldly qualifications such as wealth or titles but in Christ the priest in whose priesthood the Catholic priest participates in a special way.[49] Hence, the Church states the following:

> Thus, the identity of the priest comes from the specific participation in the Priesthood of Christ, in which the one ordained becomes, in the Church and for the Church, a real living and faithful image of Christ the Priest, "a sacramental representation of Christ, Head and Shepherd." Through consecration, the priest "receives a spiritual 'power' as a gift which is a participation in the

authority with which Jesus Christ, through his Spirit, guides the Church."[50]

Thanks to this identification of the priest with Christ, the former is specifically inserted into the mystery of the Trinity. What does this mean? It means that through ordination, the priest is placed in "a particular and specific relation with the Father, the Son and the Holy Spirit," a relation that far surpasses the communion with the Trinity, which is received at Baptism. For the priest who is a visible continuation and sacramental sign of Christ in his own position before the Church and the world is "inserted into the Trinitarian dynamics with a particular responsibility." In fact, priestly identity has its ultimate origin in the love of the Father who sent his Son, our high priest and good Shepherd, in whose priesthood the ministerial priest participates and to whom he is united through the action of the Holy Spirit. Thus, "the life and the ministry of the priest are a continuation of the life and action of the same Christ." Here then is the true identity of the Catholic ministerial priesthood, its true dignity, and the fountain of joy of priests.[51] This explains the joy and happiness of many priests—as Father Barnabas and other priests showed today

This priesthood, unlike the priesthood of the Old Covenant, is not inherited or transmitted from one family member to another. It neither originates in the Christian community nor derived from delegation from the community. Rather, every priest is a gift of Christ to the community; he is an ambassador of Christ and his representative before the people entrusted to his care.[52] The power committed to him at ordination is not human but from God. Jesus assures him of this when he said, "As the Father has sent me I also send you;" "He who listens to you listens to me."[53] Yes, Jesus has chosen his priests and appointed them to work for him. They continue on behalf of Christ and his Church the priestly work of the Savior and eternal priest. Christ acts through each priest, and the liturgical acts of the latter are the acts of Christ and the Church. When, for instance, Father George baptizes, it is Christ who baptizes, when Father Eusebius absolves from sin, it is Christ who absolves, and when Father Jude celebrates Mass, it is Christ who celebrates.

The sacrament of orders not only gives to the selected men called to the priesthood the grace proper to this sacrament, but also confers an indelible mark or character that shapes its recipients to the image of Christ the priest and enables them to perform their dual duty of sanctifying men and glorifying God. Thus, this sacrament sets priests apart from all other Christians, endowing them with supernatural power so that whatever they bless is blessed and whatever they consecrate is consecrated.[54] Is this not an amazing honor? That the almighty God should condescend and choose ordinary, weak men and elevate them to this unbelievably exalted position, the place of Christ in the Church! It is really amazing! Many people cannot indeed take it in. Many saints see the priesthood as more sublime than any other vocation or profession. They regard it as an astounding miracle, greater than any human dignity, and should be numbered among the things of heaven. For they see the priest as inferior only to God and superior to man. And it is their argument that the entire world or the whole Church without a priest cannot give to God as much honor "nor obtain so many graces, as a single priest celebrating a single Mass." This is so because the Mass is the sacrifice of the Cross, which is of infinite value, worth more than the sacrifices of everybody and everything in the world. The gift of priestly dignity surpasses all human understanding.[55] This is why a priest who accepts chieftaincy and secular titles, except academic or professional titles, exhibits his ignorance of the dignity of the priesthood that he has received. The beneficiary of such a gift should always be very grateful to God for the great gift. He should see his choice for this noblest of callings as a sign of divine love. Like many of those chosen by God, as we see in biblical tradition, he should not forget at all that ordinarily, he is unworthy of the vocation. He should therefore serve God in gratitude and humility.

The Call and Its Challenges

Daniel: Thank you, Father. But how does a person know quite well that he has a vocation to the priesthood? And do priests have problems?

Fr. Paul: These are important questions, though I cannot give all the answers now. I shall endeavor to give some important ones today.

In the Bible, we notice that those specially called by God to work for him usually have a deep sense of their unworthiness. It is, for instance, seen in the call of Isaiah, that great prophet whose writings foretold most of the mysteries in the life and death of Christ, and who is sometimes called the fifth evangelist. When he was first called to the prophetic ministry, he had a vision of God seated on his throne and surrounded by a throng of seraphim or angels who were singing and praising the holiness of God. They sang thus: "Holy, holy, holy is the Lord of hosts; all the earth is filled with your glory." Just like Isaiah, the first major feeling of the one called to serve God is a sense of the presence of God, a sense of the holiness of God, a sense of the otherworldly, the unworldly. This is not often dramatic and needs to be directed. The one whose interest in the priesthood begins with a sense of the earthly dignity of the priesthood or worldly attractions to that vocation needs a good spiritual or vocations director to put him on the right track.

The reaction of Isaiah at this vision reveals the usual second reaction or feeling of the one called. Upon seeing the holiness of God, Isaiah noticed the unbridgeable chasm, the yawning space or gap between the God of holiness and sinful man. Hence he cried out, "Woe is me, I am doomed! For I am a man of unclean lips, living among a people of unclean lips; yet my eyes have seen the King, the Lord of hosts!" This is a feeling of one's sinfulness, a true sense of unworthiness. The candidate is amazed, even shocked, that God should call him to a vocation so exalted, considering his weakness and unworthiness. God hardly works with those who are full of the sense of their own worthiness and importance. But he usually works with people who know their unworthiness and their need of cleansing. As Isaiah was cleansed of his uncleanness by a seraph who took a burning coal from the altar, so also those called by God to work for him are usually cleansed. This cleansing may begin in the seminary or even before the seminary and goes on through life. It comes in various forms, such as sickness, deprivations, privations, betrayals, false accusations, mental anguish, unmerited suspicions, and misunderstanding. Other forms may be working with implacable neighbors, coworkers, or very difficult parishioners or circumstances. All these are means of cleansing the candidate to make him fit for the call or vocation.

The third moment or stage in responding to God's call is usually the actual answer. Isaiah answered, "Here I am, send me."[56] On the day of ordination, the candidate answers, "I am present." This is the expression of his willingness to accept the call and do God's work. Not very long after his ordination, he may begin to feel the weight of the cross that he has accepted. The vocation to which he has been called is so sublime, ordinarily beyond the reach of human beings. But he knows his own weakness, his own unworthiness, and his frailty. Considering the frailty of his human nature vis-à-vis the sublimity of his vocation is a heavy cross for the priest. He is called to a vocation far beyond his natural powers, and yet he has unceasing warring of the flesh and the longing for the world that beckons on him and sometimes even seems to force him to conform to its standards or demands. In whatever situation, however, the priest must not forget that response he made on the day of his ordination. His response, "I am present," is equivalent to Isaiah's "Here I am, send me." It means readiness and willingness to carry the cross and to work for God despite one's unworthiness. Every priest in time of difficulty or trial in his vocation should renew his commitment with such expressions as "Lord, I am ready and willing" or "I am present." These expressions not only renew his commitment on the day of his ordination, they also remind him that he made his commitment before God and the world. In so far as he is making the real effort to do God's will, he should not be discouraged by his weakness or trials. It is clear that God does not call angels to be priests but men, who have human nature with its assets and liabilities. And even when Jesus chose the apostles, he did not choose perfect men or men who were thought to be worthy; he rather chose common folks. It was through his compassion and mercy that he made them more worthy. If he calls a man to be a priest, it is out of his special love for the one called, not because that man is worthy or lovable.[57] Therefore, priests should always trust God and cooperate with him and his grace.

No matter what happens, the priest should not despair as long as Christ is with him. This is one of the lessons to learn from Peter's miraculous drought of fishes.[58] In that incident, Peter and his companions had worked very hard through the night, trying to catch some fish, but they caught nothing. However, in broad daylight, Jesus, who had finished teaching the people, told Peter to go back and try again. This time, he was not to repeat the past mistakes but to correct the lapses or imperfections of the past. Peter obeyed the Master and began again, not counting the many times he had tried and failed. Unexpectedly, this time he succeeded and in a big way. He caught too many fish for his boat alone to haul to the shore. The priest must remember this when he is tempted to despair. He should bear in mind that his vocation is not immune to mistakes or failures. For instance, he may notice that despite his self-denials, he is often still tempted; that despite his efforts to control his emotions, his feelings often betray him; that despite his efforts to pray well, he still cannot pray like a saint; that despite all his efforts for the growth of the faith of his parishioners or flock, he notices a lot of lapses or even betrayals by the very people he is devoting his life to help or save. In such situations, he should not forget that, like Peter, he is being summoned to begin again in his response with faith and hope. One failure or two is not the end of the world. There was a saying we learnt in our primary school days: "Try, try, try again and never give up." The priest should put that saying into action and never give up because of failure, persecution, or other difficulties.[59]

When he has made good and honest effort and yet sees himself not making much progress, he should never give up. He should rather remember always that he who called him does not leave him to fight alone. His wars and even his failures will fulfill God's purpose for him[60] provided he is doing his best to do God's will. His many trials and tests, his agonies, tears, and frustrations are not wasted. At the end, he will see that they served God's purpose and that they helped to shape him into what God wants him to be.

Now let us continue on the miraculous catch of fishes. Peter had labored all night without success. Jesus told him to try again; he obeyed. He succeeded this time and excellently, beyond all expectations. As an experienced fisherman, why should he go fishing in broad daylight when he failed at night, which was a better time for fishing? Like Peter, the priest must learn that obedience and reliance on the Master are keys to success. He must find out that the most successful moments of his life as a priest are the times when he has a deep, sincere relationship with Jesus. Jesus especially reminds priests of the necessity of this relationship for their success. "Without me you can do nothing,"[61] he warns. A priest can easily forget this as he does his priestly assignment.

Seeing that this astounding catch of fishes at the Lord's direction was beyond human power, seeing it clearly as a miracle, as God's special intervention, Peter perceived the difference between his human weakness and the enormity of God's power revealed in Jesus. He had to declare, "Depart from me, O Lord, for I am a sinful man." After this miracle, he saw the divinity in Jesus; hence he called him this time Lord instead of Master. Here we can see that the reaction of Peter is similar to the reaction of Isaiah when the latter was called by God as we saw above. It is the same sense of the revelation of the presence of God and one's unworthiness, which always accompanies every genuine vocation to the priesthood. For the candidate is surprised or rather overwhelmed that God should bestow such a great favor on him in his nothingness. This is the attitude of the creature before the creator, of man before God. Confronted with this sense of his own weakness and unworthiness for the vocation, the priest should be consoled by the description of the priest in the Letter to the Hebrews: he is a man chosen from among men to be their representative before God; like other people, he has his own weakness and must offer sin offering for himself and for the people.[62]

However, even though the priest has to know that he is not superior to those among whom he works or to whom he preaches; that he is not as learned as some of those he has to instruct or direct, he must always be aware of his position as a special servant of God, as a representative of Christ, and to rely on the Master. Christ can use him, despite his weakness, to achieve his purpose. All he asks of us is to lend him ourselves including our weakness, and he can use us to surprise even us. We learn from the Scriptures that Jesus borrowed many of the things he used. He borrowed Peter's boat to preach, borrowed an ass on which he rode into Jerusalem for his passion, borrowed the house where he took the Last Supper with his disciples and instituted the Blessed Eucharist (and even borrowed his grave). He made good use of all that were loaned or lent to him. So also will he make good our loan to him.[63]

Causes of Joy and Gratitude

I suppose, continues Fr. Paul, you have learned something more about the priesthood today. Now, let us consider some of the things in his ministry that should make the priest happier and more grateful to God for giving him this vocation. His ministry as priest accompanies the Catholic throughout the latter's lifetime. He confers the sacrament of baptism on the newborn child; a few years later, he instructs the child and prepares him for the reception of the Holy Eucharist and confirmation. He endeavors to bring back to God the sinful members of the faithful by preaching and the sacrament of penance and reconciliation by which he forgives their sins. Men and women entering into Christian marriage kneel before him to receive his blessing. In serious sickness, he is called to the bedside to pray and anoint the sick person for healing or to help him make a final preparation to go back to God. So, from birth to the final moment of the Catholic on earth, the priest is needed.

This need of the priest in the most important aspects of the Catholic's life has been expressed by the prayer and praise of the priest's hands.

> We need them in life's early morning, we need them again at its close;
>
> We feel their warm clasp of true friendship, we seek them when tasting life's woes.
>
> When we come to this world we are sinful, the greatest as well as the least.
>
> And the hand that makes us pure as angels is the beautiful hand of the priest.
>
> At the altar each day we behold them and the hands of a king on his throne
>
> Are not equal to them in their greatness, their dignity stands all alone;
>
> For there in the stillness of the morning, 'ere the sun has emerged from the East,
>
> There God rest between the pure fingers of the beautiful hands of the priest
>
> And when we are tempted and wander to pathways of shame and of sin,
>
> 'Tis the hand of priest will absolve us—not once but again and again;

And when we are taking life's partner, other hands may prepare us feast,

But the hand that will bless and unite us is the beautiful hand of the priest

God bless and keep them all holy for the Host which their fingers caress;

What can a poor sinner do better than to ask Him, Who chose thee to bless?

When the death-dews on our eyelids are falling, may our courage and strength be increased,

By seeing raised o'er us in blessing the beautiful hand of a priest![64]

One may ask here, but why is it that only the hand is given so much praise and attention in the priest beginning from his ordination? And why is it that the priest's hand is anointed during ordination? The hand being anointed is a sign of the Holy Spirit and his power. For the hand represents the whole human person. It is, says Pope Benedict XVI, "the instrument of human action, it is the symbol of the human capacity to face the world." At the ordination of priests, the bishop lays his hands on the candidates for ordination. It means the Lord himself has laid his hand upon them and wants their own hands so that they may become the Lord's in the world, to serve him in the world. He wants the priests' hands "to be instruments of service, hence, an expression of the mission of the whole person who vouches for him and brings him to men and women . . . anointed hands must be a sign of the human capacity for giving, for creativity in shaping the world with love." For this reason, the priest is always in need of the Holy Spirit. The priest should always put his hands at the Lord's disposal and pray to him to continually take him by the hand to lead and guide him. Faith in Jesus is the means through which this can always be accomplished. It is the duty of the priest to pray that he be never separated from Christ or his Body. For the Lord has made every priest his friend and representative. He entrusts everything to his priests; he entrusts himself to them, so they can speak with his own authority.[65]

This helps to make a priest be trusted by many. We know that in modern society, many people often take few people into confidence, especially in things that matter much to them personally or to their families. But often it is not so with the priest. Both the young and the old usually prefer to go to him for advice and consolation rather than to any other professional. In many cases, he is taken into confidence in personal, sensitive matters. Many people, whether individuals, groups, or families, disclose to him confidentially what they may not disclose even to their close relatives or friends. In places where the doors are closed to many, they open for the priest. Often he seems to be a member of every family while actually belonging to none. Why is this so? Why is it that some people trust him so much and look to him for the solution to their problems? This is because they see him as very close to God. Hence, they request Masses and ask for the priest's prayers. That is the reason they send him as their ambassador before God to thank him on their behalf for his favors, to ask for forgiveness for them when they offend him, to express their continued loyalty to him as their king, and to plead for them for their needs.[66] Indeed, the priest is the last hope of the people in time of suffering or crisis. This was demonstrated not long ago at the remote African village of Umuncha.

Here, a petrol and gas station accidentally caught fire. The workers tried the fire extinguishers available, but the fire was too much for them. The firefighters, who were tens of miles away, were contacted by phone, but they were slow in coming. Meanwhile, the fire was raging horrendously, threatening to spread to the surrounding residential buildings. The proprietor of the petrol station and his workers were desperate and helpless as they watched the source of their livelihood go up in flames. But perhaps more desperate were the people whose homes were threatened by this inferno. They gazed helplessly since they could do very little at that very time to stop it from spreading. The local parish priest whose attention was drawn to this rare and disturbing spectacle in his community drew near to find out what was happening. As soon as the desperate people saw him, they rushed to him, pleading that he should come to their homes either to pray there or to stay with them during the whole length of that disaster. They were convinced that the priest's presence and prayer would help keep the fire away from their homes.

But do not think that attitude, the attitude of seeing the priest as very close to God, is limited to Africans. It is not; even though many Africans love and respect their priests very much, the attitude of seeing them as very close friends of God is not limited to them alone. For instance, not long ago in an international flight taking off from New York, there was a woman in her thirties, probably American or European, who was scared to death of flying in an airplane. A priest who was taking the same flight checked in a little later. The attention of many in that vessel was drawn by the shout of the lady as soon as she saw the priest come in. "Thank God, Father is here," she cried. She was reassured that no harm would befall all in that trip because the priest was with them.

Even many non-Catholics have great trust in the Catholic priest. That trust enabled a priest a few years ago to dissuade a man from committing suicide. This man, raised a Protestant, seemed to have given up all religion. In the turmoil of a serious disagreement with his family, he quietly left his New York home with the intention of committing suicide to escape from the family worries. On his way, the place he was heading to carry out his intention was a Catholic church. When he reached there, he paused a little, stared hard on the edifice, and continued on his way. Just that time, a priest stepped out of the rectory and met the man. With a smile, he greeted the man. The man, with a nod, forced a smile back to the priest, and after taking a few more steps, he stopped and asked the priest, "Could I speak with you for a moment?" The priest warmly welcomed him and took him to a quiet room in the rectory, where the man poured out his anguished heart to this priest who did not know him and had not met him before. The priest patiently listened and at the end of three hours (9:00 p.m. to 12:00 midnight) that summer night, he offered his counseling to him. It was only then that the man told the priest what had been his intention. He was going to commit suicide when providence made him meet this priest. He thanked the priest for listening to him and talking him out of his former wicked plan. The priest had, in turn, to thank God and continues to thank him for making him a priest whom any person or group, irrespective of religious affiliation or color, could trust and speak to confidentially.

There are surely many more things the priest has to thank God for. Greatest among these is the power to act in the person of Christ, *in persona Christi*, in the Church, especially in liturgical celebrations, doing things considered as prerogatives of God himself. An example is the power to forgive sins. The Jews are right in insisting that no one can forgive sins but God. Jesus proves to them that he is God and that he has the power to forgive sins.[67] With the words "Receive the Holy Spirit; if you forgive the sins of any, they are forgiven, if you retain the sins of any they are retained,"[68] he gave this power also to those who take his place in the Church, his priests. According to Saint Alphonsus Liguori, if Christ were to descend into a church and sit at the confessional to administer the sacrament of penance, and a priest to sit at another confessional in the same church to administer the same sacrament, the penitent of each would be absolved.[69] And Saint John Vianney, *the Cure of Ars,* while full of love and respect for the Virgin Mary, remarks that neither she nor any angel is given the power to forgive sins, but a priest, no matter how simple he is, is given this power. Reflecting on the dignity of the priesthood, the saint says that the priest cannot understand in this life but in heaven the greatness or height of his office. "If he understood it on earth, he would die, not of fear but of love."[70] He also says, "If I were to meet a priest and an angel, I should salute the priest before I saluted the angel. The latter is the friend of God; but the priest holds His place. St. Teresa [of Avila] kissed the ground where a priest had passed."[71] Considering his own weakness and unworthiness, should the priest not be bewildered or rather shocked that God should single him out and entrust so much power and responsibility to him?

But the greatest privilege or blessing of the priest is in his power to celebrate the Eucharist. By the power given to him by Christ, the priest has the privilege of presiding at Mass, of bringing about the Eucharist: when at Mass, he pronounces the words of consecration, and the bread and wine are changed into the Body and Blood of Christ. At his bidding, Jesus comes down substantially to the altar. This is a great miracle. That alone can show the unbelievable honor and power given to the Catholic priest. At Mass, Christ offers himself again and again to the eternal Father through the priest's ministry. Here, especially, the priest sees the dignity of his calling. For without him there will be no Mass, no Eucharist. Christians would be badly starved spiritually. Reflecting on the importance of priests and the dire need of them in the world, especially for the celebration of the Eucharist, Pope John Paul II makes the following moving appeal to priests:

> Dear brothers: you who have borne "The burden of the day and the heat" . . . who have put your hands to the plough and have not turned back . . . and—perhaps more especially—those of you who are in doubt about the meaning of your vocation or the value of your service, think of the places where people anxiously await a priest and over the years of waiting have never ceased to hope for one. Sometimes they meet in an abandoned shrine and place on the altar a stole which they still keep. They recite all the prayers of the Mass until they come to the words of consecration. Then a deep silence comes upon them, a silence sometimes broken by a sob . . . so ardently do they long to hear the words that only a priest can speak effectively. They long for Holy Communion, for which they depend on the ministry of the priest, just as they also

long to hear the words of pardon: *Ego te absolvo a peccatis tuis*. How deeply do they feel the lack of priest. There are such places in the world.[72]

Saint John Vianney, the Cure of Ars, makes an important observation when he says that when people wish to destroy religion, they begin by attacking the priest, "because where there is no longer any priest there is no sacrifice and where there is no longer any sacrifice, there is no religion."[73] The continuance and growth of the Church would be disturbed without the celebration of the Eucharist. For these depend much on the Eucharist, so without the Eucharist, the Church would cease to exist. Indeed the Eucharist is the source and summit of the Church's apostolic work. It will be useful to highlight this privilege by considering a little here the importance of this gift in and for the Church. The Eucharist is at the root of the Church's foundation and its celebration. Among the other things, it is the renewal of the covenant of Calvary. This necessarily leads us to see briefly here the notion of covenant in the Bible—to authenticate that statement.

A covenant, according to the Bible, is a solemn ritual agreement by which each of the parties involved solemnly binds itself to be totally committed to the welfare of the other party just as it is committed to its own. This is to say, by a covenant, the parties exchange not only their interests but also their persons. Hence, covenants were used in marriage agreements and other serious agreements or pacts. Usually after a covenant, a very close bond is created between the covenanted parties. Thus, typical covenants created families or communities similar to families. There were ritual blessings for the keeping of the covenant and imprecations or curses for its violation. The seriousness of a covenant is indicated by the fact that it was ratified or sealed with blood. The blood not only represented the creation of a blood relationship or bond between the parties but was also a warning or a reminder to each of them that the first to break the terms of the covenant would suffer the fate of the victim whose blood was used in the covenant. That is to say, that party should die or suffer the imprecations invoked in the covenant. It is interesting to note that the same curses or blessings redound on the parties who later renew a covenant even if they were not present when the covenant was originally made. Let us keep this in mind as we now consider actual covenants.

In the book of Genesis, God made covenants with Noah and Abraham. But the covenant that definitively made Israel belong to God in a special way was the covenant of Sinai. By this covenant, God made clear the choice of the nation of Israel as his special people. The nation becomes God's special possession, a holy nation, a kingdom of priests. This implies that Israel will act as mediator between God and other nations or peoples.[74] Moses splashes the blood of the covenant on the altar representing God and on the people reminding them that it is the blood of the covenant.[75] This is to show the establishment of a union between God and the people. It was this covenant that created or constituted the Israelites into the People of God.

However, the covenant of Sinai was a type and prefigurement of the covenant of Christ, which he started at the Last Supper and completed on Calvary. Through this supper and covenant, Jesus founded the new People of God or the Church. According to the New Testament narrations of the institution of the Eucharist, Jesus has in mind the making of a covenant, for all four sources have it that he gave his disciples the cup as the blood of the covenant.[76] Luke and Paul make it clear that it is specifically the new covenant long foretold by the prophets,[77] for both in the accounts state thus: "For this cup is the new covenant in my blood." Thus, according to the New Testament accounts, through this ritual communal meal, which is the symbolic action[78] of his death together with the anticipated death and resurrection, Jesus effected a new covenant between God and his new people, thereby creating a new saving community, the new People of God, the Church. Just as the covenant of Sinai ratified with blood made the Israelites the old People of God, even more so the new covenant, sealed with the blood of Christ, makes the new Israelites (Christ's followers) the new People of God (new family of God) or the Church. Thus, the renewal of this covenant in the celebration of the Eucharist continues to build up the Church by making salvation available to the faithful and promoting unity among believers. Hence, the Second Vatican Council says, "As often as the sacrifice of the Cross . . . is celebrated on the altar, the work of our redemption is carried out. At the same time in the sacrament of the Eucharistic bread, the unity of the faithful, who form one body in Christ . . . , is both expressed and brought about."[79] The Eucharist thus builds the Church, the Church that makes the Eucharist, and if there were no Eucharist, the Church would cease to exist. But thanks to Christ who has blessed the Church and the world with the priesthood and Eucharist. Saint John Vianney puts the priest next in rank after God, higher than the angels. He says that if he were to meet a priest and an angel, he would salute the priest first before saluting the angel. For a priest can successfully say Mass while an angel cannot. And where there is no priest, the Church dies.[80]

Daniel, my dear, there are a lot of things to talk about; indeed we cannot find words enough to thank God for his goodness in choosing us to be his priests. As we noted above, the priesthood belongs essentially only to Christ by nature. But out of love for us, he chose us to participate in his ministerial priesthood and to represent him in the Church. Now, since we are participators in something that is not ours by nature or by right, it is reasonable that we should be very close to Christ in whose priesthood we participate. This is necessary if we wish to be priests according to his own mind. In other words, we have to be special friends of Christ. Christ himself makes this demand. To his priests he says, "You are my friends."[81]

He lays down, as a prerequisite for our success, closeness to or friendship with him as we hinted above. Says he, "As a branch cannot bear fruit all by itself, but must remain part of the vine, neither can you unless you remain in me. I am the vine, you are the branches."[82] Here Jesus sums up what participation in his life and priesthood entails. As life and food come from the tree to its branches, so does our spiritual life as Christians, and especially as priests, come from Christ. To be healthy spiritually then, to be the type of priests he wishes us to be, we have but to be close to him; we have to be his friends.

The Second Vatican Council calling this friendship perfection or holiness sees it as obligatory for every priest, since the latter is Christ's representative and instrument for uniting men with God. It maintains that this holiness contributes immensely for success in the priestly apostolate. "Priestly holiness contributes very greatly to a fruitful fulfillment of the priestly ministry. True, the grace of God can complete the work of salvation even through unworthy ministers. Yet ordinarily God desires to manifest his wonders through those who have been made particularly docile to the impulse and guidance of the Holy Spirit."[83]

Not long ago I was in a gathering of a few priests where this topic was the main subject of the discussion. Some asked a number of questions that may be summed up in these short remarks or questions: How possible is it now to think seriously of becoming friends of Jesus when the habits formed in the seminary do not fit in with life in the parish; when the things that used to appeal to me have lost their fervor; when the interest I anticipated in handling the Blessed Sacrament did not last long; when the hearing of confession has become a very weary work, and the thrill of giving absolution has disappeared; when there is so much work in the parish that the priest has hardly any time for himself? There could be an endless list of questions or reasons why a priest should give up friendship with Jesus. These reasons or objections may be verbalized or not. But common sense and the Church have made us know that every priest is bound to aspire to be a friend of Jesus. Friendship is the first thing that Jesus demands from every priest. He has said that his priests are or rather should be his friends, not his servants.[84] So, he will not be satisfied with only service if a priest does not offer him friendship. No matter what fruits we gather, Jesus will not be satisfied unless we produce some fruit ourselves. Far from belittling the hard work of the priest, this statement means that the priest's hard work will be more acceptable to Jesus if he himself is first of all close to the Master.

Without this, the priest may gain little from his own labor. It is true that Jesus chooses priests for the salvation of human beings, but we must not forget that he chose us first of all to be his friends. He may not accept whatever we offer to him if we refuse to give him our heart. This is verbalized in these words: "Whatever you offer to me besides yourself, I account as nothing; I seek not your gift, but yourself. Were you to possess everything in the world except me, it could not satisfy you; so neither can anything you give me be acceptable without the gift of yourself. Offer yourself to me and give yourself wholly to God; so shall your offering be acceptable."[85] This friendship will help us to build the all important living image of Jesus in our mind and keep that image fresh and effective in our lives.

"I Will Take the Cup of Salvation"

Daniel, you also asked whether a priest can have problems. Surely, like any human being on earth, the priest must have problems at one time or another. I have indirectly mentioned some of them when I was describing the priest and his life. However, before we begin to look at some of these problems more closely, it is better we recall once more some of the blessings of the priesthood.

We have seen, thanks to his vocation some of the privileges given to the priest by God. The greatest of these are the power *in persona Christi* to forgive sins and the power to change bread and wine into the body and blood of Christ in the celebration of the Eucharist. These powers are far beyond any human creature. Yet they are given to the priest. Sometimes a priest can forget the fact that his vocation is a great gift. He should not take it for granted. What should be the priest's reaction or response? I suppose it should be one of humility and gratitude. Thinking about his vocation should give him enough material for reflection at least some days in the month.

A priest should sometimes ask, "Who am I that I should be the one chosen from among many people who are better than I am in my family, my kindred, village or neighborhood, town or city, state, country and even in the world? Why is it that among the many young men who started with me in the seminary, I am one of the few chosen to be priests? Did I deserve it? How? I, in no way, deserved it. It is a divine mystery. I know from all eternity God had me in his plan. Then in his own time he created me and called me from my mother's womb."[86] This is the Lord's doing, and it is wonderful in our eyes.[87]

What sometimes enables the priest to take in why he was chosen is considering the pattern or way God chooses as seen in the Bible. He does not choose those who are worthy in the eyes of the world. He chooses the weak to confound the strong.[88] Thus, he chose Moses, a fugitive and stammerer, who objected to his choice with this question: "Who am I that I should go to Pharaoh and lead the Israelites out of Egypt?"[89] In the same way, he chose Gideon, who confessed that his clan was the weakest in Manasseh and that he himself was the smallest in his family.[90] So also was the choice of David, who was considered the least or not even qualified to be king of Israel.[91] Jeremiah objected to his call to the prophetic ministry with the cry, "I do not know how to speak; I am a child."[92] In the New Testament when Jesus chose his disciples, he did not choose the cream of the population but common people; most were fishermen and one a tax collector, who was therefore considered a sinner. Paul was chosen when he was persecuting the Church. This litany shows that God chooses out of his love and plan. He has special love for the priest. That was why he chose him. I am a priest simply because God has special love for me.

What then shall I render to the Lord for all that he has done for me? I can do nothing but take the cup of salvation.[93] What is this cup? Saint Augustine says it is a bitter cup, the cup of suffering in imitation of Jesus, who took his own cup in obedience to the Father's will.[94] It is the sum total of the sufferings that the priest encounters in his life and ministry as a priest. Accepting the priesthood is accepting the cross. We know that the last phase of Jesus' saving ministry started with his agony in the garden of Gethsemane. There he envisaged all the sufferings that he would undergo if he persisted in the obedience to the Father's will, his decision to take the cup of suffering. Here the weakness of his flesh was tempted to rebel, to reject that cup. If he did that, the salvation of the human race would have been jeopardized. By his "Yes" he reversed the "No" of our first parents; by his total obedience to the Father he countered the disobedience of the first human beings on earth and thereby brought about the salvation of man. Christ's yes at Gethsemane cost him the whole way of the Cross which ended on Calvary. The priest who takes the place of Christ in the Christian community should be ready to imitate his Master and accept his own cup, his own sufferings. Doing that is treading on the path that our Savior has blazed for us.

These sufferings are many and varied. In the first place, we priests should remember that when we answered the call, we undertook to uproot the kingdom of the devil and to establish or spread the kingdom of Christ. In other words, we declared war against the devil. And we must be sure that the devil does not fold his arms and watch his kingdom being destroyed. He will use everything at his disposal to fight back. This is one of the sources of the troubles for those who work for God, and we should not forget it. Sufferings or troubles of this nature are not peculiar to priests but common to all who work seriously for the growth of God's kingdom. Nor does a priest simply work to please people but God. In thus serving God diligently (for the Gospel he preaches goes contrary to the life and way of the world and worldly), he will surely annoy some people, especially the powers that be. These often react to prove their power and authority. It is naive, therefore, for any priest to think he is going to be the darling of everybody or that his ministry will be pleasing to all. He must do all he can to serve God and the people entrusted to him without unnecessarily intending to offend anyone, but he should not expect to be praised by everybody. Other problems such as loneliness, hatred by the world and the worldly, betrayals, deprivations, etc., can be heavy burdens also. But the priest faces them or carries the cross or cup out of love for God. Any priest who loses the sense of the carrying of the cross for love of Christ will find the priestly life very burdensome and uncomfortable. The conviction that they are accepting or carrying the cup for love of Christ is what fills missionaries with zeal and sustains them in any type of adversity or suffering.

Consider, for instance, the first missionaries to come to our land. They took the risk to go to an unknown very distant land. On their arrival, the language barrier, the racial differences, and the suspicion of the natives of their intention all posed difficulties for them, so nobody cared to listen to them. They were not discouraged. Seeing the suffering of the people, they forgot their own. The first thing they did was to buy slaves from slave ships. These slaves they set free. They also gathered orphans and outcasts and took care of them. They traveled long distances on foot along winding pathways through thick forests, always exposed to the dangers of wild animals, wicked men, and suspicious chiefs. One of them, Bishop Shanahan, walked from Onitsha to Cameroon, a distance of more than 350 miles in 1918, to evangelize there.[95] The greater cause of fear and worry was the alarming death toll of the missionaries. Between 1886 and 1900, a period of only fourteen years, the missionaries, few as they were, lost ten of their colleagues owing to malaria.[96] The survivors persevered amidst these sufferings and deaths. Their great desire to evangelize the people ultimately started to pay off. For the people could see their selflessness and their love for the natives. They therefore accepted their preaching and teaching. The missionaries continued their work under difficult conditions until they prepared the people through education and evangelization to win their independence from colonial rulers. They held the batten of evangelization in our land until our civil war. Daniel, you were not born by the time of the war. The missionaries remained and faced all the dangers and sufferings of war with our people. What enabled them to do this was, I think, their love and gratitude for their vocation. They accepted their cup with equanimity. Do you know the earthly reward they received for all their work in our land? They were forcefully deported by the government immediately after the war. But before then, they had handed on the batten of the Lord's commission to the native clergy. The native clergy themselves rose to the occasion. They were very few in number. For instance, in the then Owerri diocese, only twenty-four priests were available to man fifty parishes and various other Church institutions. The case of these missionary and the native clergy is a good illustration that a priest, for all his labors and sufferings, is not to look for his consolation or reward here on earth. Like Christ, his Master, he accepts his cup or cross for love of God. This cup may be very bitter, but it will not be too bitter for a faithful priest because he is convinced God is with him. Sometimes, despite its bitterness, the cup gives the priest joy for he relies on God. Hence, he calls upon the name of the Lord as he carries the cup (*et nomen Domini invocabo*). Indeed, being a faithful priest is like pouring one's life like a libation to God. At the end of this earthly ministry, a priest will be happy to declare with Saint Paul, "My life is being poured away as a libation, and the time has come for me to be gone. I have fought the good fight to the end; I have run the race to the finish; I have kept the faith; all there is to come now is the crown of righteousness reserved for me, which the Lord, the righteous judge will give to me on that Day."[97]

Daniel: Thank you, Father, I have learnt much today. Please, could I meet with you again on Wednesday? For there are other matters I would like you to clarify for me.

Fr. Paul: Let me check my diary. Thursday would be better for me. I am free on Thursday. See you then.

Daniel accepted the appointment. At this time, they arrived at the home of Fr. Barnabas's father and joined in the feasting.

✝

Chapter 3

The Priest and the Eucharist

As was stated in chapter one of this book, the death of Christ on the Cross was his chief high priestly act. And the Eucharist is the re-enactment or renewal of that act of Christ on the Cross and of the Last Supper. Hence, the Eucharist is the chief high priestly work of Christ continued in the Church. It is the great sacrament of our worship of the Father, the central or principal mystery of saving worship in the Church. It contains all the spiritual treasure of the Church, as the Second Vatican Council clearly states, "The other sacraments, and indeed all ecclesiastical ministries and works of the apostolate are bound up with the Eucharist and are directed towards it. For in the most blessed Eucharist is contained the whole spiritual good of the Church, namely, Christ himself . . . . For this reason the Eucharist appears as the source and summit of all preaching of the gospel."[98] Hence, the Eucharist should be the center of the life and ministry of the priest.

Although other sacraments of the Church are saving mysteries or means of grace, they derive their efficacy from the Eucharist and are directed back to it as the summit of the Church's liturgy. In fact they revolve round the Eucharist as the planets of the solar system revolve round the sun. Let us now briefly see how. Through baptism, a person is initiated into the Church, the People of God, the people whose praise and thanksgiving to the Father reach their zenith in the celebration of the Eucharist. Confirmation strengthens one so as not to withdraw from this Eucharistic people and from the Eucharistic sacrament. And it may be interesting to note here that these two sacraments, together with the Eucharist, constitute the sacraments of initiation. Penance usually forgives sin and thus reconciles and reunites the sinner with the Eucharistic People of God and enables him to participate in the Eucharist once more. By the sacrament of the anointing of the sick, the Eucharistic People of God commends those who are ill to the glorified Lord that he may raise them up and save them. It also prepares the sick for receiving Communion and strengthens the Christian to persevere as a faithful member of the Eucharistic people during the ordeal of suffering.[99] Christian marriage on its part is a symbol of the union between Christ and his Church, a union that is expressed and celebrated in the Eucharist, the sacrament of Christ's total self-giving.[100] We shall consider the relationship between the Eucharist and orders in a moment.

Thus, the Eucharist, the reenactment of the redeeming sacrifice of Christ pours out the abundant fruits of this sacrifice to men through the other sacraments. The centrality and importance of the Eucharist in relation to other sacraments is underscored by the fact that the Church now very much encourages that, whenever feasible, the celebration of each of these sacraments should be done within Mass. In addition, the blessing or consecration at the Chrism Mass of the oils used in the sacraments of baptism, confirmation, holy orders, and the anointing of the sick clearly shows the pride of place the Eucharist enjoys among all the sacraments.

Now, if all the other sacraments are closely related to the Eucharist, the relationship and closeness of the Eucharist with holy orders is unique. Holy orders, or rather the priesthood, exists essentially for the Eucharist. The Eucharist is the raison d'être of the priesthood. Both sacraments were instituted at the Last Supper, and the Church commemorates their institution at one ceremony on Holy Thursday. In fact, the first priests of the new Covenant were automatically ordained when Jesus at the institution of the Eucharist said, "Do this in memory of me."[101] Moreover, it is possible to celebrate the other sacraments outside of Mass, but from the early history of the Church ordination to the priesthood (including the diaconate and the bishopric) is always within the Mass. What is the point for all this elaboration? It is simply to show that the priesthood derives from the Eucharist and exists for it. A priest may be a theologian, an explorer, a journalist, a poet, etc. But none of these occupations identifies him as a priest; presiding over the celebration of the Eucharist surely does. The Church states it clearly: "The priest fulfills his principal mission and is manifested in all his fullness when he celebrates the Eucharist."[102] Therefore, priests should be quite aware that they exist in a special way for the Eucharist, the great treasure of the Church entrusted to them. Indeed, without the Eucharist, there would be no priesthood, and conversely, without the priesthood, there can be no Eucharist.[103]

The foregoing statement looks so simple. But we need to reflect on it. The faithful or People of God join in the offering of the Eucharist by virtue of their common priesthood, yet it is only the ordained priest who, acting *in persona Christi* or in the person of Christ, can bring about the Eucharistic sacrifice and offer it to God in the name of the people. That is why, in the Catholic tradition, only the ordained priest recites the Eucharistic prayer, "while the people participate in faith and in silence."[104] *In persona Christi* does not simply mean in the name of Christ, but it means "in specific sacramental identification" with Christ the High Priest and author of the Eucharistic sacrifice or the Mass. Says Pope John Paul II, "The ministry of priests who have received the sacrament of Holy Orders, in the economy of salvation chosen by Christ, makes clear that the Eucharist which they celebrate is *a gift which radically transcends the power of the assembly* and is in any event essential for validly linking the Eucharistic consecration to the sacrifice of the Cross and to the Last Supper." For a valid Eucharistic celebration in a Christian assembly, an ordained priest must preside over the celebration. The ministerial priest is a gift to the community given to it *"through episcopal succession going back to the Apostles."*

Thus, nobody else—no king, no queen, no scientist, no genius, nor a whole nation or even a combination of a group of nations—but an ordained priest can bring about the changing of bread and wine into the body and blood of Christ. And there can be no Mass or celebration of the Eucharist without a priest.[105] And no Catholic community can be built "unless it has its basis in the celebration of the Eucharist."[106] Therefore, there is no Catholic church if there is no celebration of the Eucharist.

As Pope John Paul II points out, just as the Eucharist is the center of the Church's life, so also is it the center and summit of the ministry of the priest. Nowadays many priests are involved in a variety of engagements or occupations. Some are psychologists or psychiatrists or teachers or engineers or scientists, etc. In the midst of all these tasks or engagements, it is easy sometimes for a priest to lose his focus. That is why the Church insists that it is important for the priest to counteract this danger and to help the growth of his own spirituality through the Eucharist, which is the center and summit of the priestly ministry. He must endeavor to celebrate the Eucharist daily, "even if the faithful are unable to be present, it is an act of Christ and the Church."[107] A priest who loves his priesthood should endeavor to say Mass every day. Love of the Eucharist is very important for him and those put in his charge. He must be aware that the Eucharist is a touchstone of faith and also of the degree of the priest's love for Jesus and his Church. We remember that in the eleventh century, precisely in 1079, a priest theologian Berengar (or Berengarius) had serious doubts about the Eucharist. He did not pray for faith but started to express his doubts by his speeches and writings. He was summoned by the pope to make a proclamation of faith. The Eucharist was thus his stumbling block instead of a means and center of his priestly life and ministry. This could be true of any priest who loses his faith in this great mystery of faith, the Eucharist. The Eucharistic sacrament and sacrifice helps the priest to grow in faith and love, if he really has love for it, celebrates it with due reverence according to the rubrics of the Church, and encourages the faithful to love it. But on the day he begins to take the Eucharist for granted or begins to celebrate Mass as mere routine, on the day he begins to see the Mass as his personal property in which he can make changes according to his own wishes or desires, on that day too does his priesthood begin to slide backward, and if he does not revive his faith, reverence, and love for this great mystery, he may deal his vocation a ruinous blow. The Church both warns and admonishes the priest who thinks he himself can make changes in the liturgy, especially in the celebration of the Mass with these words:

> He cannot consider himself a "proprietor" who can make free use of the liturgical text and of the sacred rite as it were his own property, ... At times this latter might seem more effective, and it may better correspond to the subjective piety; nevertheless, objectively it is always a betrayal of that union which should find its proper expression in the sacrament of unity.[108]

In celebrating the Eucharistic sacrifice every priest should always remember that the approved liturgical text is an expression and representation of the Church's unity.[109] Priests owe it as a special duty, therefore, to have a great reverence for this sacrament and, through their own witness and veneration, not only help their own spiritual growth but also build up the spiritual life of those entrusted to their care. In his homily at the ordination ceremony in Rome on April 29, 2007, Pope Benedict XVI said to the deacons to be ordained priests, "To be his ministers, you must ceaselessly nourish yourselves with the Eucharist, source and summit of Christian life. In approaching the altar, your daily school of holiness, of communion with Jesus, of the way of entering into his sentiments in order to renew the sacrifice of the Cross, you will increasingly discover the richness and the tenderness of the love of the divine teacher, who today is calling you to a closer friendship with him."[110] Priests should indeed be in love, on fire in their own veneration and their desire to promote similar devotions in others. Any priest who is not devoted to the Eucharist should not be surprised if his spirituality and ministry suffer, since the Eucharist is the beginning, means, and end of the priestly ministry, since "all ecclesiastical ministries and works of the apostolate are bound up with the Eucharist and are directed towards it."[111]

Thanks to the centrality of the Eucharist in the life and ministry of the priest, it is also the center of the pastoral promotion of vocations. The priest's diligent celebration and devotion to the Eucharist, together with the active and fruitful participation of the faithful, help to promote vocations by offering sincere young men example and incentive to respond to God's call. I have seen priestly vocations actually inspired in some young men by a priest's diligent celebration of the Eucharist. At one occasion, one of the factors in the priest's celebration that aroused the curiosity and interest of the boys was the priest's inspiring homily. After Mass one morning, these boys met the priest in the sacristy and asked him a question that expressed this curiosity. The question was this: "Where does the priest get all that he says during the homily?" The priest told them that if they became priests, God would give them the wisdom to speak for God. With their curiosity thus aroused, they decided they would become priests when they grew up. Both priests and other Catholics should, through the celebration of the Eucharist, promote vocations. This appeal is more urgent these days of scarcity of priests in the West. For it is distressing for a Christian community that is big enough to be a parish but cannot because a priest, who is the only person qualified to offer the Eucharist, is lacking. Sometimes when such situations arise, some religious and lay people may help in various ways, such as the Sunday service without a priest or even Communion service, but these must be seen as temporary measures while the community awaits a priest. This absence of the priest should be an incentive to the faithful to do all they can to promote vocations to the priesthood, "without yielding to the temptation to seek solutions which lower the moral and formative standards demanded of candidates for the priesthood."[112] And here it is important for us priests to remember that out of his immense humility and love for us and the world, the Lord Jesus has surrendered himself to the custody of priests in the Eucharist. He has confidence that priests will protect him and his glory in this great sacrament. Sometimes, however, it is observed that some of us forget this trust when, instead of carefully choosing suitable and trusted parishioners to serve as extraordinary ministers of the Eucharist, we leave it open for any parishioner who wants or volunteers to participate in this ministry. And some of these sometimes take Communion to the sick and homebound. In this case, is it not possible that some enemies of the Church can, with evil intention, become Christians and volunteer to be extraordinary ministers of the Eucharist? They could pretend to take Communion to the sick while in fact their real intention would be to insult or abuse Jesus in the Blessed Sacrament by intentionally desecrating it. Should we cooperate in this grave sin by allowing Our Lord to be thus insulted by his enemies?

The Mass, the Priest's Sacrifice

In chapter 1 of this book, we stressed the fact that the essence of the priesthood belongs to Christ alone, the one mediator between God and man. There too we spent some time discussing the importance of interior disposition in sacrifice: that without interior disposition, the disposition of the heart, the external rite is reduced to empty hypocrisy, which is displeasing to God. For interior disposition is the very essence of sacrifice and not an accessory to the rite. We noted that Jesus' sacrifice was first and foremost an interior disposition, or rather interior sacrifice, a sacrifice of obedience to the Father's will. It was actually this interior disposition, as we noted, that made Jesus' death on the Cross a sacrifice and pleasing to God. For God is not a cruel father who must be placated by the most humiliating death of his Son on the Cross. What rather makes the sacrifice of Christ on the Cross pleasing to the Father was that on the Cross, Christ's lifelong total obedience to the Father's will reach its highest point. That was why, in the midst of his anguish on the Cross, he breathed his last with the words, "It is consummated." It was a cry of triumph in which Jesus rejoiced that he accomplished the task of remaining faithful and obedient onto death and fulfilling the Father's will. This surrender, or rather Jesus' total obedience, even onto the death on the Cross, is what gave his death a sacrificial and saving value. If he did not have this total obedience or surrender at that crucial moment, his death would not have been a sacrifice. And it would not have been salvific. But thanks to his interior sacrifice, the external sacrifice has great meaning and saving value. And through it, the world has been saved.

Now, as we already know, the Mass is the same as the sacrifice of the Cross. When therefore we celebrate the Mass, we offer again to God the exterior and interior sacrifice of Christ. Let us now consider this in relation to the priest's own act and life.

When the priest celebrates the Mass, he acts *in persona Christi,* in the person of Christ, as another Christ. Here he must have the same mind as in Christ.[113] He must mean what he says. Since he, in the person of Christ (*in persona Christi*), celebrates the same sacrifice in which Christ's surrender of his own will to the Father's will reached its highest point, the priest must make Christ's interior disposition his own not only during Mass but also through his whole life. He must allow this disposition to permeate his own life. What does this mean? It means that the priest should expand and apply the sacrifice he offers to the whole of his life and dispositions. He must endeavor or at least seriously desire to live as Christ lived. He must endeavor to offer also his own will to God. Otherwise, his sacrifice with regard to himself would be similar to sacrifices of the Old Testament priests who offered something rather than themselves to God.

We must remember that were the priest to attempt to undertake this commitment by himself without supernatural help, it would not be possible. He should rely on and trust in God. The very sacrifice he offers gives him the communion or union with Christ, the means and strength to succeed in this holy undertaking. He can say with Saint Paul, "I can do all things in him who strengthens me."[114] It is not reasonable, therefore, for a priest to see himself as merely a person who brings people to God by preaching and ministerial work, but for whom growth in his spiritual life through his ministry is not essential. God forbid that any priest should see himself as merely a pipeline through which graces and blessings pass but retains none for himself. He is not free not to grow in his close relationship with God through his ministry. The very sacrifice he offers dedicates or devotes him as completely to God as Christ himself. Therefore, the priest's daily Mass—as far as he is concerned—is a deliberate lie if he does not make efforts to live close to God, which is a life of sacrifice.

I suppose the last sentence needs more explanation. As noted above, the Mass can be the priest's sacrifice, yet it is not his own property. It is the act of Christ and of the Church. The priest, as a minister of Christ and of his Church whenever he celebrates Mass, no matter his disposition, if he intends to celebrate, he celebrates validly.[115] But what fruit does he reap from his own Mass? The value of the Mass, as applied to the priest, very much depends on his own disposition. He can gain little or nothing in his own sacrifice if his own life and interior sacrifice do not, in some way, correspond to what the Mass stands for. In ordinary life, it would be considered a serious illness if a person every day prepares food for others to eat but cannot eat the food he prepares. By this I do not mean that the priest does not receive Communion (because the Mass is not complete without his Communion). I rather mean here that if others are gaining from perhaps his ceremonially beautiful Mass while he himself gains little or nothing from it, he is starving to death while feeding others fat. To put it in another way still, if the priest's life and interior disposition do not correspond with what the Mass says, those of the Christian faithful who participate in these Masses with interior recollection and sacrifice gain from the Masses while the priest himself goes away empty. Is that not lamentable? Most priests may not be able to count the number of Masses they have celebrated since their ordination. Counting them is not important. But as far as their spiritual life is concerned, how much have they gained from all those Masses?[116] The priest must therefore not take the Mass for granted. Before every Mass, he must pause, reflect, and resolve to offer himself anew. I suppose one of the reasons for the prayer for vesting before Mass is to remind the priest of this. And that is also one of the reasons silence should always be observed in the sacristy.

As is clear, our main concern in this particular reflection is to determine what the life and disposition of the priest should be in view of the fact that he celebrates Mass. The Mass reenacts the sacrifice of the Cross and makes it ours; this sacrifice is the perfect expression of Christ's life and disposition. Therefore, if the Mass is to be truly our sacrifice, we must live in such a way that it is also an expression of our own life. This statement may look dry or artificial. Let me make it a little clearer. It implies that we should offer ourselves at every Mass with the bread and wine—at the offertory or preparation of gifts. As we do this we should accept in advance all that God's will permits to happen to us during the day, and we should endeavor to spend the rest of the day with this disposition. We may sometimes, during the day, forget this resolution, but we should renew it as soon as we remember. If we do this faithfully and consistently, our life will ultimately be an expression of the miracle that takes place at Mass. We know at Mass we present to God bread and wine, work of human hands, natural things. But God, in his omnipotence and love, changes these natural things into supernatural things. He changes them into the body and blood of Christ. Similarly if we really offer ourselves at Mass and mean what we say, God will accept us as an offering and consecrate us; he will transform us and incorporate us into Christ, our high priest and leader. This transformation and incorporation is one of the reasons Christ left his body and blood as food and drink so that he may live in us and we in him.[117]

But again we have to remember that the consumption of Christ's body and blood is made possible because a sacrifice had taken place: Christ's own sacrifice. In consuming the food and drink of this sacrifice, we imitate the victim that we consume at the sacrifice. We have to sacrifice ourselves also to God; otherwise, we do not mean what we say. My pledge at the consumption should be, "As Christ offered himself to God and became a sacrifice for us, I also offer myself to God and abandon my affairs to him. Let him do with me what he will." Many dioceses nowadays, especially in Africa, have ordinations to the priesthood every year. In each of those ordinations, the bishop tells the candidates for ordination, "Know what you are doing, and imitate the mystery you celebrate: model your life on the mystery of the Lord's Cross."[118] By these words the Church reminds its new priests that the Mass they will now begin to celebrate is the sacrifice of Christ on the Cross and that their life should be modeled according to that sacrifice, that is, according to the sacrifice of total dedication and surrender to the Father's will.[119]

In his apostolic letter for the 2004, year of the Eucharist, Pope John Paul II emphasizes the connection between the consumption of the body and blood of the risen Christ and mission. It gives "an urgent summons to testimony and evangelization" to both the Church and every Christian. Referring to Saint Paul's teaching, the pontiff stresses the close relation between the Eucharistic meal and proclamation. Entering into communion with Christ in the Eucharist carries with it "the duty to be a missionary of the event made present in that rite." In fact, the Mass gets its name from this sense of mission. The English term *Mass* is a translation or transliteration of the Latin word *Missa*, which the celebration of the Eucharist came to be called because of its missionary implication. At the end of the Mass, the priest says to the congregation *"Ite Missa est"* (when the dismissal is in Latin), which means (by the Eucharist you have celebrated) you are now sent on a mission into the world. Thus the dismissal at the end of each Mass is "a *charge* given to Christians, inviting them to work for the spread of the Gospel and the imbuing of society with Christian values."[120] The Eucharist itself provides the interior strength for this mission since receiving it is receiving Jesus, who strengthens the Christian for this work. For this to happen, however, each Christian must "assimilate, through personal and communal meditation, the values which the Eucharist expresses, the attitudes it inspires, the resolutions to which it gives rise."[121]

He must also assimilate the meaning of *Eucharist*, which comes from a Greek word meaning "thanksgiving." It is so called because in Jesus, in his sacrifice, in his unconditional surrender to the Father's will, is contained the "thank you" and the "amen" of all humanity. When we celebrate the Mass or the Eucharist, we must remember that we, with and on behalf of all humanity, are saying "thank you" to God for what he has done for us and the world through Jesus Christ, especially in his death and resurrection. This attitude should not end at Mass, however; It should be in mind always and should animate our thoughts and actions everywhere.[122] It is good for every priest to assume as his disposition before Mass the good advice attributed to Monsignor Knox: "Priest of God, celebrate this Mass as if it were your first Mass, as if it were your last Mass, as if it were your only Mass."

Eucharistic Devotion outside Mass

Eucharistic devotion outside Mass includes Eucharistic procession, Benediction of the Most Blessed Sacrament, the Holy Hour, forty days' adoration, and more. But here I wish to concentrate only on the Holy Hour.

A few years ago, Fulton Sheen was a household name in most Catholic families, especially in the United States. Indeed, Archbishop Fulton Sheen was one of the greatest orators and writers that the twentieth century produced. Though very well educated, he attributed his success as orator and writer more to his devotion to the Eucharist than to his education. He did the Holy Hour every day of his priestly life that spanned a period of sixty years; he never missed it even for one day of those sixty years. He explains that, on the day of his ordination in 1919, he made two resolutions. One of these was to do the Holy Hour every day. He kept that resolution till the end of his life in 1979. This archbishop gives three reasons why he kept the resolution. The first was that he saw the Holy Hour not simply as a devotion but rather as a sharing in the work of redemption. By our Holy Hour, he says, we join in the work of reparation to combat evil. The second reason was that the Holy Hour was the only request Jesus made of the Apostles throughout his company with them. "Could you not watch one hour with me?" Jesus needs the company of his friends, especially priests, who act in his person in the Church. He wants them to spend an hour of silence and love with him, not an hour of activity, but an hour of listening and loving with him in the Eucharist. The third was that he wanted to grow more and more like Jesus through company with him.[123]

I suppose it will be useful for us to reflect briefly on each of these three points. It is indisputable that Archbishop Fulton Sheen helped his people to grow in faith. Almost thirty years after his death, tapes of his talks are still selling like hotcakes in America and are regarded as treasures. Thanks to his preaching of the Holy Hour, many people who strayed or were falling away from the Church regained their faith and came back. Not only Catholics, but also Protestants, were attracted to his beloved practice of the Holy Hour. His aim of helping through devotion to the Eucharist in the work of redemption is thus fulfilled.

Archbishop Fulton Sheen was not the first to realize the power of the Eucharist in the conversion of souls. Long before him was a French priest, Curé d'Ars, the Parish priest of Ars, who marvelously bore witness to the power of the Lord to convert souls through this mystery of faith. When John Mary Vianney arrived at Ars, he found out that though many of the people were baptized Christians, most of them were living as unbelievers. One of his first steps was worshipping Jesus in the Blessed Sacrament for many hours. He rose very early in the morning, about 3:00 a.m., and prayed before the Blessed Sacrament until broad daylight, when he then celebrated Mass. There he continually requested Jesus to convert his unbelieving parish. After Mass, he continued his prayers in the church. At this early period, those who wanted to see him did not need to go to the rectory but to the church.[124] He continued in this way for some time. At first nothing seemed to happen. But he was not discouraged. But then, not very long, his prayer started to be answered. The faith and conversion of the parish started to grow by leaps and bounds. Soon, not only the whole of France but also many people from other countries of Europe started to flock to this priest in the remote village of Ars, seeking spiritual help and direction.[125]

This was a priest, who by human standards, was considered not very bright, who found his studies in the seminary very difficult. He was actually sent to the remote village of Ars because the place was obscure. He was not considered suitable for the city parishes lest his perceived ignorance would disgrace the Church. But he was a wise man. He knew his weakness and also his strength. His strength was his strong prayer life, especially his devotion to the Eucharist. This made the great and the small leave the learned priests in the cities to come to him in his remote village. Even many priests and bishops sought his spiritual help.[126]

The second reason for the practice of the Holy Hour is that it was the only request Jesus made of his apostles throughout the course of his stay with them. This company with him must be important to Jesus not only for the salvation of the world but also because he desires the friendship of his followers, especially his priests. Today he is repeating the same request: "Could you not watch one hour with me?" Shall we refuse him this time? With the following words, Pope John Paul admonishes priests and the religious to be frequent in their adoration of the Eucharistic Jesus outside Mass: "Called by that very consecration to more prolonged contemplation: never forget that Jesus in the tabernacle wants you to be at his side, so that he can fill your hearts with the experience of his friendship, which alone gives meaning and fulfillment to your lives."[127] The pontiff also invites the clergy, the religious, and the lay faithful to "take the time to kneel before Jesus present in the Eucharist, in order to make reparation by our faith and love for the acts of carelessness and neglect, and even the insults which our Savior must endure in many parts of the world. Let us deepen through adoration our personal and communal contemplation."[128]

The third reason for the Holy Hour is obvious. Stated in another way, it says that nearness affects us. For instance, friendship grows stronger by the friends coming closer or keeping close contact. When iron is put in the fire for a long time, it often assumes the color and nature of fire. Fire changes it to fire, so to speak, because it is in fire. So also our nearness to God or nearness to Jesus in the Blessed Sacrament affects us. Recall the case of Moses coming down from Mount Sinai, where he had been for some time with God, conversing with him. His stay in the presence of God for this considerably long time made his countenance begin to shine even though he himself did not notice it at first. His face became so bright that the Israelites could not look at it; it was too bright for them. For their sake, Moses covered his face with a veil when he wished to be with them.[129] The countenance of Moses was transformed into a brilliant fire because of his prolonged stay in the presence of God. That is a lesson for us. If we too resolve to stay in the presence of God the Son in the Eucharist, if we make the Holy Hour a daily exercise for a good part of our priestly life, God will surprise even us and transform us into what he wants us to be.

We can see this verified in the life of the patron saint of parish priests, Saint John Mary Vianney. His great miracle, the transformation of Ars, was so famous and enduring because he himself was first transformed. He became very holy and was endowed with supernatural gifts that attracted many people to him. Again, we see such a wonder in the life of Archbishop Fulton J. Sheen himself. He attributed the power of his many writings and speeches more to his devotion to the Eucharist than to his great education. He wrote his speeches and books before the Blessed Sacrament and usually preached his retreats before the Lord in the Blessed Sacrament.

These two men, John Vianney and Fulton Sheen, were priests like us. They resolved to succeed despite all odds. One of the most powerful and unfailing ways they followed was the way of enduring devotion to the Eucharistic Jesus. Surely, we too wish to succeed as priests. Let us then follow their example; let us resolve today to do the Holy Hour every day. And let us keep that resolution. We may complain of lack of time. If we mean it, time will surely come. It may need our giving up perhaps an hour of our sleep in the morning. If we persevere in this, we shall reap the reward even starting in this life. Almost every pope of the twentieth century recommended the Holy Hour or rather devotion to the Eucharistic Jesus. Why do we not start today?

Some who are not acquainted with the Holy Hour may wonder what one has to do before the Blessed Sacrament for a whole hour. However, if they begin, they will find out that sometimes one hour becomes very short. A person can have his mental prayer or say the Rosary or even the Office of the Hours there.[130] That can form part of our Holy Hour. But we have to know that the most important thing in Holy Hour is listening or rather conversation with Jesus who is present in the Eucharist. We have to listen to him with the ear of our mind. This is difficult and even impossible if we are not sincere in our friendship with Jesus; if we do not mean what we say; if after telling Jesus we love him, we join his enemies to strike him, to go contrary to his will; if in our relationship we seek ourselves, not him; and if we love inordinately any created being—man or woman or anything. In other words, we cannot surely converse with Jesus if we have an idol, that is, if we have any created thing that takes the first place in our lives.

✝

CHAPTER 4

Clerical Chastity and Celibacy

D aniel met Father Paul according to their agreement. Without wasting time, Daniel thanked him for the appointment and fired his first two questions.

Daniel: I have two questions. First, is it a sin for a seminarian to have a girl as a friend? Second, should a priest love women?

Fr. Paul: Let me now answer your first question.

This question may look simple, but there is need for some explanation before any answer here. I suppose you have been given some sex education in the seminary.

Daniel: We have not yet received much sex education in the seminary. Most of the time, what they tell us is to keep away from girls and women. The only people who talk much about sex education are some of our lay teachers who tell us that if a man fails to know a woman, he will either go mad or fall into a serious illness.

Fr. Paul: This is a serious lie and pure deception. It is not true. Many priests are happy and healthy even though they have been celibate and chaste all their life; they have not known any woman. I hope that the seminary will make arrangements to teach you balanced sex education and should not allow anybody to mislead you. For without proper education in this matter, you will find chastity an intolerable burden in your priestly life.

I suppose the seminary authorities wish to tell you for the moment to keep away from occasions of sin; that is why they are telling you to beware of your relationship with girls and women. In the near future, I hope they will teach you more. Yes, you should know more. Those preparing to be priests should be quite sure about these matters for their own good and that of those they will teach. Even before you are given formal seminary teaching on sexuality, you should learn much from your reading of the Bible, especially the letters of Saint Paul. Paul admonishes us all to know how to use our bodies in a way that is "holy and honorable, not giving way to selfish lust like the pagans who do not know God," for God usually "punishes sins of that sort."[131] He reminds us that through baptism, our bodies are no longer ours as such but belong to Christ. Hence, an act of impurity by a Christian is a very serious offense, since in such an act he defiles not simply his own body but also the body of Christ; he drags the Son of God himself into prostitution. For him this is shocking. He goes further to say that through the same baptism, our bodies too have become the dwelling place of the Spirit of God, temples of the Holy Spirit. A sin of impurity is thus not only dragging Christ's body into prostitution, it is also defiling or rather destroying the temple of God.[132] And he warns that "if anybody should destroy the temple of God, God will destroy him, because the temple of God is sacred."[133] Thus, Saint Paul makes it clear that our bodies are made for the glory of God. God receives this glory when our sexuality, our body, is disciplined to stay in harmony with the will of God.[134] This is the meaning of chastity. It is "regulating the use of generative faculty according the principles of reason and faith" or regulating the use of this faculty to give glory to God.[135]

Let us, for a moment, keep the Bible aside. But let me now give you a small tip of sex psychology. This may lead to your first question.

Or after that, you may be able to find out the correct answer to that question. Now, let me begin with sex attractions and true friendship.

Sex attraction. Every normal human person is a social being and a member of a definite sex. As such he or she has a natural desire for companionship and innate attraction toward the members of the opposite sex quite different from the attraction they have toward the members of their own sex. This is sex attraction, and it is varied. But it can be reduced to only three main types, namely general sex attraction, physical sex attraction, personal sex attraction.[136]

General sex attraction is the general attraction toward the members of the other sex. Its common characteristic is that it is not directed toward any purely physical satisfaction and not centered on any individual but consists mainly in a strong interest in the members of the other sex and their distinctive qualities. Women, for instance, are especially attracted by the courage, strength, and energy of men. Men, on their part, are attracted by the tenderness, grace, and beauty of women. Each sex is attracted to admire those qualities, which are especially distinctive of the members of the other sex. Each experiences an inborn desire to hear the voice of the other, to be with the other, and to see the other. Each too experiences a natural desire to know more about the distinctive qualities or characteristics of the other. This natural sort of mystery about the other sex has a God-given purpose. For it draws the sexes together in social life, makes them know their mutual power over and mutual dependence on each other, and finally leads to marriage and prolongation of the human race.[137]

It is necessary here to point out that when the God-given gift of sex attraction is not properly managed, it can be a source of danger to chastity. For instance, when a man's mind is constantly on women, or when a woman's mind is constantly on men, then there is a danger of moving to actual impure action. Or when curiosity about the other sex crosses the bounds, such as when it leads to unnecessary readings or to pornography or when it leads a person to try to see more and more of the body of the other sex, it easily becomes a source of physical stimulation and hence a danger to chastity. Curiosity about sexual matters is quite a peculiar kind of curiosity different from most others. One can safely light a cigarette around the seashore or in the open field. But he cannot do so at an active petrol filling station. If he does, he risks the danger of causing a fire that he cannot control. Such is the curiosity about sex matters. This is why the Church condemns many modern methods of sex education, which often lead to the arousing of sexual impulses, the management of which is often not easy. Therefore, common sense is much required.

Physical sex attraction. Now let us touch briefly here on physical sex attraction. This type of sex attraction seeks the other sex as a means of stimulating and satisfying carnal passion. It therefore impels one to such acts as will afford the desired satisfaction, mainly to passionate, intimate embraces and ultimately to carnal knowledge. Human beings share this type of sex attraction with animals. It should be properly managed; otherwise, it can be a great source of disturbance.[138]

Personal sex attraction. Generally, in the life of a boy or a man, he usually likes girls or women or he is attracted by many of them, but he has a special attraction toward one. Girls and women have a similar experience with regard to boys and men. This special interest in or attraction to a particular individual is often a specific indication or rather manifestation of a sexual instinct known as personal sex attraction. This type of sex attraction has strong emotional manifestations as one of its characteristics. Probably the most distinctive mark of personal sex attraction is its exclusiveness or monopoly. The person thus attracted wants total ownership or possession of the beloved. The mere idea that the beloved might feel some attraction toward another person results in a strong feeling of jealousy. Such a lover is aware that his own emotions have been totally charmed or captivated and that he has almost no inclination toward others. He therefore wants the same response from the one he loves, that is, complete monopoly of her love or affections. If by chance two men have this type of attraction toward one woman, it can lead the two to a serious disagreement or quarrel. Conversely, if two women have personal sex attraction toward one man, it can lead to an open fight.

Personal sex attraction is certainly an emotional fascination. The other person or party is seen not simply as good but rather as wonderful. How this type of attraction starts is often a mystery. Sometimes there is a gradual buildup to this affection; at other times, it just happens suddenly and unexpectedly. However, when it happens, it is based on the discovery of one or more of the qualities or characteristics that attract one sex to the other, only that now these characteristics have suddenly assumed a sort of personification in this one man or woman. The basis of attraction might be a person's masculine or feminine attitude to life, strength, tenderness, voice, walk, etc. Whatever the basis, this affection goes straight to the heart and is very strong.[139]

The absence of the beloved even for a short time is hard and creates a feeling of dissatisfaction and a yearning for her presence or company. This is expressed by frequent and emotional letters or phone calls. It must be noted here that this affection is not satisfied with mere presence of the beloved. It tends to show itself by sweet or sugary words, protestations of love, and physical contact such as kisses. And if this type of affection is mutual, then the hearts of both parties are locked together; they tend to like or dislike the same things. They want to share everything together. Both are convinced that this state of affairs will last forever.[140]

Personal sex attraction is designed by God to lead to marriage, and within marriage, it is a wonderful help to a happy, stable, and holy married life. But since it locks the hearts of two persons completely to the exclusion of others, outside of marriage, it is a social nuisance. This means that it can cause a lot of trouble and ridicule to two persons who fall into this type of love and are not married or do not intend to marry in the near future. Personal sex attraction, however, like most other emotions, is blind. Often it works without reason. It does not look for a person's compatibility or virtue. It may go out to one who is not eligible for permanent companionship such as marriage. Examples are numerous. It can go out to a thief, a drunkard, a criminal, a person already married, a person too old or too young, etc. It must be directed away from the wrong person to the right person, especially from the beginning when the signs are noticed.[141] And evidently, persons who are not eligible for marriage or persons who cannot marry, such as priests and seminarians, should never foster this type of affection; otherwise, they will be laying an intolerable burden on themselves. Now, suppose a seminarian has a girl as a friend, as your question suggested, and this type of relationship develops, what happens? Do you not see that the seminarian has carelessly invented problems for himself? This is one of the reasons the authorities of the seminary tell you to beware of your relationship with girls and women. Those who pay attention to the strengths and weaknesses of personal sex attraction will save themselves and others a lot of troubles.[142] Now, let me say something about true friendship, which may help more to answer your questions.

True friendship. To have a good friend and be one, you must know what friendship is. What is true friendship? It is different from the sex attractions we have already seen because it is not based essentially on emotion. It is not mere emotional fascination or infatuation. Nor is it a companionship of mere convenience that breaks up once the convenience no longer exists. True friendship can be styled a companionship of mutual self-sacrifice. It has some peculiar characteristics. Among these, true friendship must be morally helpful; there is good basis of agreement, and it is characterized by a spirit of mutual self-sacrifice.

Morally helpful. True friendship should positively have a good moral influence. It should be able to inspire the friend to see and imitate the goodness seen in the other party. It lifts both and brings them close to Christ or to God. In true friendship, each party should aspire to help the other to avoid sin and unobtrusively inspire the friend to the practice of virtue. This does not mean that the friend has to show the other that he is better. Nor does it mean that they have to be equal in virtue, a situation which is extremely difficult to obtain. However, it should ensure positive good coming from this relationship, or at the least that the influence of these friends is not an obstacle to the practice of virtue. But a companionship that leads to sin, to lowering of ideals, weakening of faith, to troubles of conscience, to neglect of one's duty or practice of his faith or religion, is not true friendship. A relationship or companionship that takes us backward in our spiritual or religious growth is not true friendship. Such relationship, rather than bring us ultimate happiness, leads to sin and self-destruction. Such should be discontinued without further delay.[143]

Good basis of agreement. The agreement of friendship is not artificial but genuine because true friendship is not mere fascination or infatuation. To determine if the agreement of true friendship exists, a person has to find out if there exists between himself and his friend grounds or basis for genuine harmony. It does not mean that both will always have the same natural likes and dislikes, which in fact would be ruinous to true friendship. The agreement of true friendship is rather that by which the friends agree and work harmoniously on fundamental and serious matters and harmless compromises on minor issues. Differences of opinion and taste, rather than disturb the friendship, provide occasions of diversity and enjoyable points of interaction. While it is a well-known truth that compromises are part and parcel of friendship, and while it is necessary that there must be mutual respect of divergent views and overlooking of minor faults, this must be limited to minor or small matters; it must not be allowed to touch on matters of conscience. For instance, it cannot include such fundamental matters as creed, the moral code, or religion. Compromises of that nature would violate the first principle of true friendship. All things being equal then, two friends of the same religious faith or same denomination enjoy a richer friendship than persons of different religious faiths or denominations. Why? Because they have a wider field of intimacy and harmony.[144]

Self-sacrifice. Self-sacrifice is a very essential ingredient of true friendship, and without it, no friendship can endure. For friendship involves a blending of souls, and in every blending, each element or party gives up something of itself and thus contributes to the common good. This giving up of something of oneself for the good of the friendship is self sacrifice. True friendship proves itself by deeds, not by words. And a true friend often wants to share the good things he has with his friend. But unyielding selfishness, concentration on the minor faults of the friend, suspicions, jealousies, and an unforgiving heart can easily destroy friendship and should therefore be avoided. A friend should be a source of solace in time of sorrow or trial and a resort for encouragement and sympathy in time of need. But this is not easy when the friend is in a contrary mood and would rather talk about himself. The readiness at such times to cheerfully help the friend and forget oneself is a true test of friendship, for it demands a lot of self-sacrifice. Moreover, friends should endeavor not to allow the familiarity of their friendship to blunt their thoughtfulness, which helps this friendship to grow. The effort to maintain thoughtfulness and courtesies demands constant self-sacrifice. In addition, friends should be a moral inspiration to one another. The need for self-sacrifice in friendship is summed up by the golden rule: treat your friend always as you would want him to treat you, especially in disagreements, bad moods, and misunderstandings. To do this always demands a high quality of love.[145]

You can see now that true friendship is not mere sentimentality or sense appeal but rather love with reason. It is not liking based on emotions, but love based on the goodness seen in the other.[146] Now that you know more about sex attractions and the nature of love, I throw your question back to you. Do you think it is helpful for a seminarian to have a girl as a friend?

Daniel: Father, I thought it was something light and useful, but with all the explanations you have given, I think it is better and safer for a seminarian to learn to work calmly with girls and women but not to be attached to any particular one as a special friend.

Priests and Women

Fr. Paul: What was your second question?

Daniel: The question is, should a priest love women?

Fr. Paul: That is a good question. Yes, every priest should love women. Indeed, the Church does not ordain any man priest if it is discovered in time that he hates women. Women are important children of God and valuable daughters of the Church. If the priest hates them, then who will minister to them pastorally? The priest as "Father" has all in his domain as his spiritual children. These include men and women, boys and girls. As father he should love and care for all.

You notice in Scripture that in Christ's earthly ministry, it was women who followed him on his saving journeys and provided for him and his apostles. On his way to his crucifixion, while men were beating and insulting him, women wept for him and one, Veronica, was courageous enough to defy the crowd and soldiers; she came forward to him and wiped his face with her handkerchief. And remember that it was a woman, Mary Magdalene, who was the first witness to his resurrection. There are still many good women today like those women of old. Such are ready to work with the priest for the progress of the Church and glory of the name of God.

Now, looking at your question once again, I suppose by women here you mean all females both old and young. In most cases, they form more than 60 percent of the Catholic population. Not only are they more in number, they are also usually more pious than their male counterparts. This makes them come to the priest and need his help more often than men do. Generally, women are weaker by nature and need support. If this weakness is realized and prudently managed by the priest, then he will have a strong army of followers and coworkers. But if he himself is very weak toward women, there will be a lot of trouble for him. He can cause the Church a lot of troubles and embarrassment. No matter how brilliant he is, no matter how hardworking he is, and no matter how well he preaches, a priest can achieve little for the Church if he is morally very weak. Rather than being a disciple of Christ, he can be an instrument of the evil one. Going through history and the Bible, you can see that women have helped many men to grow great. But they have also brought about the downfall of many great men, such as Samson, Solomon, Holofernes,[147] and many others. It was David's mishandling of his relationship with a woman that brought the black spot in his history. The priest will not fare better than these great men unless he is careful in his dealings with women.

One fact every priest and every sincere Christian should know is that the mass media and the entertainment industry today are mostly controlled by atheists together with hedonistic, materialistic, and selfish cooperate bodies or institutions that feed the public with sensational and immoral materials. This has very much helped to make our present age a sensate age, an age of more feeling than reasoning. It has, in no small measure, lowered the moral standard of our society. Moreover, in our age, many people have no purpose in life. Hence, a lot of them wish to compensate for the absence of full meaning of their lives by speed, drugs, and intensity of feeling.[148] And that explains too why immorality is at its worst today.

This state of affairs affects both men and women. Above I have talked well about many women. But to be frank, the world today is so immoral in many places that some women have become too used to men. Any man they see, except a celibate priest, is ordinary. Sometimes they want to induce or even force him to prove that he is a man. If any of them succeeds in pulling down a priest as a friend in the worldly sense of the word, she considers herself as having made a great achievement. You may have noticed yourself something similar to this during your yearly apostolic work; if you are not careful, you may be messed up.

A priest friend of mine living in New York City told me of a peculiar experience he had a few years before the year 2001. It was a Saturday afternoon in summer when he received a phone call. The voice seemed to be that of a very sick woman. The woman said, "I am sick and I think I am dying. Please, I wish to see a priest before I die." The priest asked for her name and address. Even though her name was not familiar, the priest hurried to the place and knocked on the door. An agile blond young woman opened the door. When the priest entered and asked to see the sick woman that needed the priest, the young woman told him to sit down for a moment. Thinking that his sitting down was to give her time perhaps to prepare the sick person for anointing, the priest was surprised that the young woman sat down near him and asked him the type of drink he would like to drink. He thanked her and said he was not going to have any drink and demanded again to see the sick woman. But the young woman started talking, and the priest listened to make out exactly what she wanted. After sometime, it became clear to him that there was no sick person there and that the young woman wanted the company of a man. The man she wanted that time must be a priest because, for her then, other men were just ordinary. A priest was more attractive to her. To get a priest was for her to win a trophy. Women like her are many in the society today, who do everything they can to seduce priests or to lead them to sin. Such women do not know that if they sin with a priest, they incur a curse that the priest accomplice may not be able to break or dissolve.

When it became clear to the priest what the woman wanted, he could no longer delay there; he jumped out and hurried back to the rectory. That incident put a lot of questions into my friend's head. One of them was this: if he himself were a woman and the woman who called the priest were a man, what would have happened? It became clear to him the type of dangers women would be exposed to if they were ordained priests as some of them have been demanding. He praised the wisdom of the Church on this issue. If women were ordained priests, who would be their guard? For we live in a world that wants to reduce everybody to the same denominator of sex maniacs.

Daniel: Father, you have said that every priest should love women. Then, why do priests not marry? Is marriage bad?

Fr. Paul: Your question reminds me of an incident during our junior seminary days. As Legionaries of Mary, three of us went for legion work far inside the town. On entering a large compound where nobody knew us, we were warmly received. However, trouble started when we introduced ourselves as seminarians from the seminary some kilometers away. As soon as he heard this, an elderly man there repeated, "From the seminary? You are those who hate marriage. You who refuse to beget children. Whom do you expect to beget children for you to evangelize?" With this type of talk, he swayed almost everybody there to his own view and dissuaded them to listen to us.

I wish to make it clear to you that marriage is not bad and priests do not hate it. Marriage was instituted by God when he created human beings on earth and gave them the command to increase and multiply.[149] Jesus himself raised it to the status of a sacrament— that is, a holy way of salvation—and commanded that it to remain indissoluble.[150] To show his appreciation of the dignity of this institution, he performed his first miracle at a wedding—at Cana in Galilee.[151] Marriage is therefore beautiful and sacred. It is a source of grace for Christian couples who receive it and live it as Christ and his Church teaches.[152]

Priests give up marriage not because it is bad but rather as something good, which they renounce for the love of Christ and the kingdom of God.

If we consider the purpose for celibacy with only our natural reason, it may not be easy for us. And it becomes a great burden when we discuss or consider it from its history, from the view that the Latin

Church at some time instituted it as a necessary requirement for its priesthood. But if we consider it from the Christological, prophetic, and missionary point of view, we can begin to see some sense in it. Through celibacy, the priest in imitation of Christ "shows in a fuller way his availability, and embarking upon the way of the Cross with paschal joy he ardently desires to be consumed in an offering which can be compared to the Eucharist."[153] Remember the other day when we were considering the gift of the priesthood, we saw that the sincere priest gladly accepts his cross or cup in imitation of Christ and as a sign of gratitude for being chosen. Celibacy should be considered as part of that cup that he gladly accepts. He offers it as a sacrifice or as a price for the amazing gift of the priesthood given to him. And by his celibacy, he bears witness to the life to come where men and women do not marry.[154] Jesus promises great rewards for those who will leave father, mother, wife, etc., for the kingdom of heaven.[155]

He also points out that there are three types of eunuchs. Some are born so; some others are made eunuchs by men. Then he speaks also of eunuchs who made themselves that way for the sake of the kingdom of heaven. He admonishes anyone who can accept the last one to accept it.[156] Celibacy is a gift. By accepting the Latin Catholic priesthood, the priest also accepts the gift—for the sake of spreading the kingdom of God on earth. It would be childish to take back from God what we vowed to him before our relatives, friends, and the world. To do so would be committing the sin of Ananias and Sapphira, who were struck dead for taking back what they vowed to God.[157] Nobody is forced to be a priest, and everyone is given time enough to consider whether he has the gift or not. If anyone who knows that he does not have the gift takes the vow, he is bringing himself the trouble he cannot manage. It is like the proverbial tortoise that in anger rejected and poured away the food set for him by his wife but turns to lick the plate from which he poured away the food. During his long years of the seminary formation, a candidate for the priesthood is given enough time to make the decision—to choose either marriage or celibacy. If he ultimately chooses to become a priest, it means he has chosen celibacy and has given up marriage or intimate relationship with women. He cannot choose both. He has to be celibate and chaste all his life.

This is not to say that celibacy is quite easy, even for those who have the gift. At the beginning, the young man taking the vow may not know all its implications or weight. But later he will, at one time or another, begin to feel it. He can overcome the problem if his love for Christ is still intact. But it becomes an intolerable burden when he loses his love for Christ. Our hearts are made to love. Before his ordination, a priest renounces intimate love between man and wife. He did not renounce this to remain without love for someone. He rather made that renunciation so that he can love Christ more—without worrying about his wife and children. As Scripture puts it, "An unmarried man can devote himself to the Lord's affairs; all he need worry about is pleasing the Lord; but a married man has to bother about the world's affairs and to devote himself to pleasing his wife."[158] If the priest's love for Christ dies or cools down, then the love for creatures takes over just as an unfaithful husband begins to set his heart on other women when his love for his wife wanes or dies. Unless he is foolish or insane, as long as he has strong love for his wife, a good husband will not have so strong an attraction to other women as to lead him to infidelity. The priest's love for Christ is similar. He should do his best always to keep this love alive.

Daniel, I wish to remind you here that celibacy is not peculiar to Catholic priests. Some other people, without any external coercion or even suggestion, have on their own accord chosen to be celibate just for a cause important to them. From your studies, you know some of such individuals. But I wish to point out only two here. They are Mahatma Gandhi and Dag Hammarskjöld. At the age of thirty–two, Gandhi, with the consent of his wife, vowed to remain celibate till the end of his life—in order to have time to serve God and give himself to work for the betterment of the lots of his oppressed people. Dag Hammarskjöld, a one-time secretary general of the United Nations, was deeply religious. As his diary, *Markings*, can show, he was a contemplative. Because of his passionate love for world peace and harmony, he remained celibate all his life, going from one nation to another to make peace.[159] If these men who were not priests could, on their own accord, take the vow of celibacy and chastity for love of God or a cause, why can priests not do the same, whose celibacy is a witness before the world to the life to come where there will be "no marrying and giving in marriage"?[160]

Means of Preserving Chastity

Daniel: Is it really possible for anyone to persevere in chastity or celibacy? If so, what is the secret behind it? I mean, what helps one to persevere?

Fr. Paul: This is a very important question. Surely, as I said before, many priests and religious persevere in keeping themselves pure all their lives. I will now tell you some of the means or helps to chastity. There are both natural and supernatural means.

The natural means include avoiding any action with self or another that can excite unnecessary impure feelings or thoughts. Avoidance also of listening to or participating in impure stories or jokes is also necessary. In addition, we must cultivate the habit of studying. Studying here does not necessarily mean studying for a degree or academic laurel. It rather means studying for the sake of studying in order to improve one's knowledge. This is a mark of a learned person. But an educated person who has not formed that habit is really half-educated. Positive study or reading good books helps to keep the mind engaged and productive rather than being idle and becoming the devil's workshop. The study here should include regular reading of the Bible and spiritual books. Such readings have good influence on the mind and psyche. If Ignatius Loyola did not read good books during his convalescence, perhaps there would not be a Saint Ignatius Loyola today. On the contrary, reading immoral books when this is not necessary is bad and can lead one astray. Bad books can destroy good characters. We should avoid them.

The good study of a person notwithstanding, however, he cannot make progress in overcoming temptations against purity if he is not disciplined, if he cannot keep his faculties under control, and if he does not develop a strong will. Among the disciplinary measures he has to take is to avoid pornographic videos, movies, or television programs that can be a source of temptation. This is the bane of the society today! Some pray to God to help them to overcome temptations against purity and at the same time engage in watching pornographic videos and television programs that can cause temptation. Such people are not serious and sincere.

Similar to pornographic materials is unnecessary company-keeping—that is, a man and woman that are not husband and wife or very close relatives spending much time together unnecessarily. This could be a source of temptation sometimes. You remember when we discussed personal sex attraction that one of the factors that can promote this relationship is spending time together often. This is also one of the lessons one learns from the movie *My Fair Lady*. Here, a famous phonetics professor, Higgins, who declares himself a professed bachelor, in his desire to educate and make useful those abandoned and considered useless, picks up a poor, dirty street woman without manners, Eliza Doolittle. He vows to make her useful. With total disinterestedness, he takes her to his home and gives her to his servants, who wash her clean. Gradually he teaches her etiquette and phonetics. Ultimately, he makes her a lady fit for a civilized society. Now that she has become a lady, what is she to do? She thinks that the most fitting man for her as husband is her professor. As the professor still insists on his being a professed bachelor and refuses to marry her, Eliza Doolittle runs away to look for other men. But when she leaves, the professor realizes that he has unknowingly got used to life with her and her presence. He therefore went out to look for her even in the freezing cold. She too has become attached to the professor. She therefore traces her way back to his home. A similar lesson can also be learned in *The Sound of Music,* where Maria and the Captain, who at first seemed incompatible, ultimately fell in love, which led to their marriage. So avoid company-keeping.

Serious prayer life and devotion to the Eucharist are important spiritual helps. No one, however strong he thinks he is, can persevere in chastity or celibacy without a serious prayer life. This includes the prayers of the Church—that is, the Liturgy of the Hours—as perhaps the starting point. We must find good ways to pray. Daniel, you must take your prayer life seriously if you wish to be a happy priest. Again, you must choose one confessor and go to confession at least once a month to him—if possible, always. Devotion to the mother of Jesus and mother of priests, the Virgin Mary, is another important help. Experience has shown that she never abandons any of her children who runs to her in need. She is "the Immaculate Conception," the Immaculate Heart and Queen of Purity. We should always seek for her assistance, especially in times of temptation. Devotion to her includes loving those things she loves and avoiding those things she would not like to do or say.

Daniel: Father, my next question is prompted by what you said a moment ago; I heard you say that celibacy is a gift and that any seminarian who knows he does not have it should not continue in his desire to be a priest. Now, if someone has impure thought sometimes, does it mean he does not have the gift of celibacy and should leave the seminary?

Fr. Paul: It is not necessarily so. You know that every normal human being occasionally can have impure thoughts. And because of the chemistry of the body, anybody can be aroused sometimes, even without a serious cause. This normal arousal is not necessarily sinful. It is sometimes a sign that the body is functioning properly and can easily be brought under control. But if a seminarian is always thinking about girls or women, if his discussions are often about them, and if he indulges in viewing pornographic videos or reading books that can easily arouse him when such reading is not necessary, he should be open to his spiritual director and follow his recommendation, even if it means leaving the seminary.

Daniel: Father, I am saturated, indeed inundated, with a lot of new information. I am very grateful to you for being so generous with your time and knowledge. All that I have learned from you will help me a lot both now and in the future. When I return to the seminary next week, I hope to share some of this knowledge with my friends.

With heart full of joy and gratitude, this young seminarian left Fr. Paul's rectory and went home.

✝

CHAPTER 5

The Woman to Love

Behind every successful man, they say there is a woman. Indeed, it is difficult to find a balanced and successful man in any conventionally accepted field of endeavor who did not have a woman play an important role in his life or in that endeavor. God, at the very beginning, saw the man's need of the support and help of the woman when he said, "It is not good for man to be alone." As it was at creation, so has been and will ever be. The priest is no exception to this rule.

But the heart of the issue here is the woman he chooses; if he chooses wrongly, he does great harm to himself and his vocation. He must therefore choose the woman who must be suitable and helpful to his vocation. Here the principles of useful companionship, or rather association, come to mind again. In other words, the suitable woman to help the priest in his vocation must be one whose association with the priest does not lead him to sin, to troubles of conscience, to a lowering of ideals, to weakening of faith, and to neglect in his religious or pastoral duties. Moreover, his association with this woman should be for him a source of sympathy, encouragement, helpful advice, and inspiration. But is it possible to find such a woman among the daughters of Eve? Only one woman certainly qualifies. Who is she? She is that one conceived without original sin and who committed no sin all her life. She is the one whom God's messenger addressed as "full of grace" and whom Elizabeth called "blessed among women"; the one who nurtured and prepared the first priest of the Christian dispensation; she who stood at the foot of the Cross as Jesus made his everlasting redeeming sacrifice on Calvary. She is Mary, the mother of Jesus and the mother of priests. The priest must come to this mother with childlike love and affection.

It is interesting to note that the first and last books of the Bible make it clear that, since the beginning, there has been a war going on between good and evil. In this war, the woman mentioned in the book of Genesis as the one who would crush the head of the serpent or overcome the forces of evil is the one who continues the war in the book of Revelation.[161] Victory is promised to her and her seed. The Church identifies her as Mary. God wants to overcome the devil not by direct divine action but rather through a human creature, and the human creature has to be a woman: Mary. On the Cross, her Son gave the forces of evil a devastating blow by offering himself as a sacrifice for the salvation of the world. It was by this sacrificial death and at his Last Supper that Jesus instituted the sacraments of the priesthood and the Eucharist. All this became possible owing to the Incarnation of the Word, owing to the fact that God the Son became man. And if we pause for a moment now and reflect, we may begin to see the role of Mary in the institution of these two sacraments, the priesthood and the Eucharist. The body offered on the Cross was the body born of the Virgin Mary *(verum corpus natum de Maria Virgine)*. Since Jesus had no human father, his entire body and blood were formed completely from the body of his mother, the Virgin Mary (though his soul was created directly by God). He received his body from Mary. Even after he was born, the food with which his body was fed and grew was prepared by Mary. There is a parallel here between the physical body of Christ and his mystical body. The growth or increase of either must come through Mary. The priest who is working for the growth of the kingdom of God, especially through the growth of the mystical body of Christ, can achieve little if he does not work in close union with

Mary, the mother of Jesus. One of his concerns is to bring all to Christ; he can hardly do this except with and through Mary. Moreover, the Eucharist or the Mass that he offers almost daily became possible owing to Mary's cooperation in the Incarnation.[162]

Especially through the celebration of this Eucharist of Jesus, the Son of Mary, the priestly ministry continues the war declared at the beginning. Thus, Mary and priests are fighting for the same cause, on the same side in the war, both fighting on the side of good, on the side of God. As it is, Mary is the highest commander of God's forces, and no one fighting on the side of God can ignore or make light association or rather closeness with her. Therefore, a wise and serious priest should accept her as mother and queen and entrust his spiritual life and whole ministry to her. Did Jesus, while hanging on the cross, not entrust the newly ordained Beloved Apostle representing all priests to her (John 19:25-27)? It would be a serious neglect on the part of any priest to reject or make light this generous gift of his mother by Jesus himself.

It was God's plan to associate the triumph of redemption with Mary. Not only did she cooperate in the Incarnation, she also suffered with her Son for the redemption of the world. She was present at Calvary, at the foot of the cross, where "she stood, in accordance with the divine plan . . . , suffering grievously with her only-begotten Son, uniting herself with a maternal heart to his sacrifice, and lovingly consenting to the immolation of this victim which she herself had brought forth."[163] It would therefore also be a serious omission if a priest overlooks the fact that Mary has an important role to play in the graces of which he is a minister. She is the mediatrix or dispenser of all graces; the graces won by her Son are distributed through her. God, who decided the regeneration of the whole human race through the New Adam, also includes the New Eve in that plan. Mary is the New Eve and mother of Christ, the Christ of Nazareth and the mystical Christ—that is, the head and members, the whole Church. The priest who is seen as *alter Christus* or another Christ cannot afford to neglect or ignore the mother of Jesus Christ. How can we be really sincere with Christ while we care little about his mother?

Devotion To Mary

Devotion to Mary is part of Catholic tradition and practice. Every sincere Catholic has some devotion to Mary. Some people misunderstand devotion to Mary as worship; that is wrong. Only God is worshipped and he alone. Devotion to Mary is an expression of filial love and honor to the mother of God and of those who sincerely love God. It is an imitation of God who himself honored her first and made Mary unique, "full of grace" and "blessed among women." Let us put things correctly right from the outset. Mary is a creature of God. Compared to him, she is nothing. The omnipotent God does not need any creature to do what he wishes. He had no and still does not have any absolute need of the Blessed Virgin Mary to manifest his glory in the world. Nevertheless, God condescended to choose Mary, his own creature, and decided to accomplish his great works through her. He continues to do so even today, for he is God and does not change his thoughts and ways of acting.[164] Each of the three divine Persons has shown his love and appreciation of Mary. This is shown as early as the Annunciation. The archangel declared to Mary, "The Holy Spirit will come upon you, and the power of the Most High will overshadow you; therefore the child to be born will be holy; he will be called the Son God."[165] Here, each of the three divine Persons is clearly specifically indicated. First, the Holy Spirit to whom the operation of the Incarnation is referred; second, God the Father whose Son is to be born; third, the child to be born, who is the second person of the Blessed Trinity. God the Father gave his only begotten Son to the world through the Virgin Mary. Says Saint Augustine, the world being unworthy to receive the Son of God directly from the hands of the Father, he gave him to Mary for the world to receive him from her.[166]

God the Son became man for the salvation of the world and was born of Mary. Jesus exalted his own independence by surrendering it to Mary in his conception, his birth, his presentation in the Temple, and in the thirty years of his hidden life. Even at his death, she had to be present so that she had to be united with him in the one sacrifice to the Father. Jesus gave infinite glory to the Father by submitting to his mother for thirty years. We glorify God too when, in imitation of our savior, we love Mary and submit to her. And the Bible makes it clear that Jesus chose to begin his miracles through her. At her visit to Elizabeth, it was by her word that he sanctified John the Baptist yet in his mother's womb. For when she spoke, John was sanctified and leaped in his mother's womb for joy. This was the first miracle in the order of grace. At the wedding at Canaan in Galilee, it was through her intercession or intervention that he changed water into wine. This was the first miracle in the order of nature. Thus, he began his first miracles through Mary and will continue them through her.[167]

The Holy Spirit formed Jesus in Mary only after obtaining her consent. He produced the Incarnate Word, God-made-man, in her and with her. He continues in the same way to produce till the end of time the members of Christ's Mystical Body. Hence, the more he finds Mary in a soul, the more powerful and effective he becomes in producing Jesus in that soul. Though he has no absolute need of her, the Holy Spirit chose to make use of her in producing Jesus and his members in her and with her.[168]

The plan adopted by the three divine persons in the becoming of man of God the Son is maintained by them in an invisible way throughout the Church, and they will continue it until the end of time. God has endowed Mary with all graces and has in fact made her his treasury. She is made the dispenser of all God's wondrous gifts. Her prayers and requests are so powerful with her Son, Jesus, that he accepts them and never rejects his dear mother's prayers. And God the Father wants Mary to be the mother of his children till the end of time. All the children of God have God as their father and Mary as their mother.[169]

From the foregoing it is pertinent then to say that to blame those who honor Mary is to blame God who initiated the practice. Anybody who reads the Bible carefully and reflectively can see that the honor given to Mary is ultimately given to God. At Mary's visitation of

Elizabeth, for instance, the elderly lady, filled with the Holy Spirit, started to pour praises on the mother of God. Mary did not claim these praises for herself. She immediately attributed all to God her savior and benefactor. Here, in her thanksgiving praises to God, she composed the *Magnificat*,[170] which now forms part of the Church's evening prayer or the *Vespers*. This is only one example. Those who think devotion to Mary is taking something away from God should start reading the Bible properly. The priest who is usually the spiritual leader of the Christian community should also be their leader in the devotion to Mary.

Mary's Coredeeming Sufferings

Before we point out a few particular devotions to Mary, it may be useful to consider her role as coredeemer. True devotion to Mary leads the priest to know both Mary's blessings and dolors or sorrows in her role as coredeemer with her son. It will also gradually lead him to the discovery of the usefulness of vicarious suffering. Often people see more the favors bestowed on Mary; they consider little the sufferings she had to undergo because of Jesus and with him. All these are mysterious plans of God for his own purpose. Now she shares in the joys and glory of her Son as she also shared in his sufferings. Did she commit any sin? But why was she made to go through all her sorrows, her *Seven Dolors*? These were her contributions to the redemption of the human race. We priests have to consider some of her sufferings and their vicarious significance so that we may imitate her and apply properly the sufferings which come to us frequently in our life and service of God.

Mary's sorrows apparently began when she brought her son to the Temple to present him to God. The old prophet Simeon told her that her son would cause her a lot of sufferings, that he would be a sign of contradiction, the cause of the falling and rising of many in Israel, and that her own soul would be pierced with a sword. Compare this to a woman taking her child to church for blessing after childbirth or churching. As the priest blesses the mother, he solemnly tells her that her child would be a great source of sufferings in her life. Surely any mother given this type of news about her child should be greatly upset. So was Mary. This first dolor or sorrow of Mary reveals to us one of the most universal supernatural principles that characterize God's dealings with those he loves much. He often allows them to suffer much on earth to prepare them for heavenly joys. For these faithful friends of his, a cross is a crown begun. That is why sufferings are dearer to the saints than earthly joys. For they have the inclinations or tastes of Jesus. They desire suffering for there is something in it that is favorable to union with God. It puts out the deceitful lights of the world, for darkness is often the light by which we can most spiritually discern God.[171]

As she was formally called upon to give her consent for the Incarnation, so now Mary was definitely called upon to cooperate with her son in the vicarious suffering for the salvation of the world. She was very generous in her acceptance of this invitation. She suffered intensely without rebellion. Her sorrows were, however, united with the sufferings of Jesus. We ourselves can make our sorrows in some way like her own by continually uniting them with the sorrows of Jesus. Happy are those whom God purifies by means of sufferings in this life. We should seek the help of Mary to be loving, sweet, and patient to those who cause us pain and unhappiness. We should request her help that, instead of thinking of revenge, we may rather think quietly of God and heaven.[172] It should be clear now that those who love Mary and wish to be devoted to her must imitate her humility and total surrender to God, her willingness to accept any suffering from him.

And every lover of God must enter into Mary's dolors or sorrows in one way or another. No one should forget that Mary's sorrows were caused by Jesus. Similarly, he will be the cause of sorrow to anyone who loves him. There are very many good earthly things we have to sacrifice to him if we really love him. Suffering must surely come to anyone who loves Jesus. It may come through unreasonable and unfounded calumnies of the worldly or in the jealousies, suspicions, and judgments of those we love; sometimes it comes from people we would least expect it from, which makes it very hard to endure. Usually, hardly is anyone left alone to serve Jesus as he wishes. The more we love him, the stronger or greater is our suffering. Jesus is the sign of contradiction, a sign set for the rising and falling of many.[173]

The weight of the first dolor was still heavy on Mary when the second one came. Though her son is the Prince of Peace, he did not have peace as his inheritance, not the peace as the world sees it. The three magi did not come back to King Herod to inform him of the whereabouts of the infant king as he had requested them. Herod had the intention to murder the child. Therefore, God in a dream instructed Joseph to flee with mother and child into Egypt. The Holy Family had to leave their home that cold and dark night without any preparation. Now they were faced with terror, hardship, wilderness, and heathen territory. Mary accepted all these with calm anguish of her sorrowful heart.[174]

Remember there were no cars, trains, or planes. They had only an ass, not a horse, for they were very poor. Therefore, most of the time, they had to march through the extensive sandy desert, which was very hot during the day and cold at night. With scanty food and drink, they were determined to reach Egypt. They did not expect miracles even though God was with them. Was not this God's own family, the Holy Family? They had a difficult and tiresome journey.[175]

At last they reached Egypt with almost nothing except their total loving trust in and surrender to God. How were they to make a start, to obtain lodging at the beginning and begin life afresh? They were typical refugees. Is it easy for a poor and unknown family to obtain lodging in an entirely strange land? What about their initial upkeep? There Joseph resumed his carpentry and Mary supported with her meager earnings. This was the lot of the Holy Family, the lot of God fleeing from the hostility and cruelty of his creatures! It was the lot of the mother of Jesus.

In considering this dolor or sorrow of Mary, it is important to remember that it was very painful to her that this sad news should be announced to her by one she loved very much—her spouse, Joseph. What about us priests? We have sometimes to announce sad but necessary news to our people and those we love. If we fail to do this, it may be a sign of immaturity or insincere love on our part for those concerned.

Furthermore, it may be fitting to state here that the cause of Mary's first sorrow was a prophecy from God; the second one was caused by the wickedness and greed of men. In our own trials, we can be more disposed to accept difficulties that are directly from the hands of God than we can accept the hardships when they come to us though the agency, the wickedness or intrigues of men and other creatures. Consider a family that lost its head and main breadwinner through an accident caused by a drunken driver, or a family that lost all it had by fire, or an innocent man who is suffering because of lies which others had invented and spread. God sometimes punishes or tries us through the injustices and jealousies of men, through undeserved suspicions of false friends, through unreciprocated love, through the ingratitude or even malice of those we have helped much.[176] We see this happening often. For instance, Archbishop Fulton Sheen tells a story of one Bishop Francis Ford, an American missionary in China. He was a good man who was very kind to his cook. But it was this Chinese cook who, in order to curry favor from the government, betrayed the bishop to the communist authorities who arrested him, handcuffed him, and had him tortured to death. This bishop, though in great anguish, accepted his sufferings as a price for the cause of Christ.[177]

Despite our holiness and bravery, we are usually inclined to shrink from the crosses that come through the hands of creatures. Even though we may know by reason that the punishment or trial is from God, it is not easy to make the acceptance convince us. For instance, the news of the death of a dear one is difficult to accept. But it becomes almost intolerable to understand that the death was caused by a head-on collision of his car with another car whose driver was a minor who had no driving license. The actions of creatures often render the source of sorrow very bitter. Like David, we wish to fall into the hands of God than into the hands of men, for God is merciful and men are cruel (2 Sam. 24:10-15). When God stands between us and the wicked world, we feel secure and grieve patiently—bending to his will. But when we are in the hands of the merciless world our anguish, our pitiable situation is greater and unpredictable. This was Mary's situation here.[178] However, even though she was suffering from the cruelty of men, she had her strong faith in God.

She and Joseph loved Jesus and accepted him as a special charge from God. For his sake they had to flee at night, in the cold and heat, marching night and day—refugees in the midst of total and suspicious strangers, Egyptians. But their main concern was his safety. To these pious souls, how painful it was to be thrust out into the desert and Egypt, where there were no synagogues, no temples, and no sacrifices to their God! They lived in an atmosphere of no true religion. Forced out of their home in the dark of the night, they had reason to be afraid of the darkness, of the marauders of the desert, of the chilling wind laden with sand that almost buried their heads in the dust.[179] All these caused them much pain. But what is more acute pain and anguish for Mary is the knowledge of the hatred men had and still have for Jesus and God. Men, even in this early history of Jesus' life, seem to be goaded by evil spirits to hate him, who took their nature to save them. We should not be surprised or discouraged if we meet people who hate Jesus and us who are his friends.

Now while they were in Egypt, although it was clear to Mary that her son was God, to other people he was as ordinary as any other child. The same can happen to us in the Eucharist, where we may lose sight of the divinity of Jesus and treat him as ordinary bread. In this consideration, it is clear that Jesus, the creator, fled from men. What about creatures fleeing from God despite all his love? As ministers of God, we must take it upon ourselves to pursue those who flee from God, capture them, and bring them to him. Their fleeing from Jesus causes him pain. It causes also pain to his mother, who shares in his pains. We must sympathize with Jesus especially for the sufferings we ourselves have caused him. We must find a way to live without intentionally offending God. If, like Mary, we truly sympathize with Jesus, we should endeavor to avoid sin. This is one of the main thoughts that come to our mind at the sixth station of the cross, where Veronica, moved with sympathy, defied the crowd and the soldiers and wiped the face of Jesus with her handkerchief. We should realize that religion is not only a matter of rules, regulations, and rites. These surely are essential. But if we perform all of them and keep all the commandments without sincere love of God, they avail us little. For the heart of religion is this sincere love for God.[180]

That is why the mysteries and life of Jesus are not past events for us. They are still ongoing. To live in sin is to chase Jesus out of his home, to put him in flight, to renew his passion and crucifixion. To live a life pleasing to God is to sympathize with him and to lessen his burden for him. We cannot sincerely do this without deep love for God. We have to go to Mary to teach us this love.[181] When we have this type of love, we are more disposed to accept any suffering from God to our own advantage. For when suffering is God's will, it is better than external spiritual advantages; rarely does anyone receive graces, except he (or others on his behalf) suffers for it.

This sympathy for Jesus helps us to learn also from Mary to aim more at compassion for others when we suffer most ourselves. This is a peculiar way of gaining graces of suffering. Grace forces us to become more considerate because we are suffering, and to go out of our way to lavish on others all the tenderness and pity that naturally we would lavish upon ourselves.[182] The grace of God and surrender to God helps us not to question the ways of God either in our own sufferings or in the misfortunes of those we love. God could have spared Mary and her family in many ways. All the circumstances of this second dolor, the flight into Egypt, seem unnecessarily aggravated. And why did God not intervene and forestall the flight altogether? These are mysteries. Greatest among the factors that made Mary's sorrows lighter was the fact that she never forgot that she was with Jesus, the light of the world. In our sufferings and grief, let not the anguish drive away Jesus from us. Rather his presence scatters the darkness. It gives us the strength to carry our burden. We, like Mary, should carry him as a little child and should not abandon him and walk away.[183]

However, Mary's pain and grief at the loss of Jesus for three days enabled her to know the pain and sorrow of sinners—people who are separated from Jesus through their own fault. Whoever has lost Jesus in one of three ways—(a) by sin, (b) worldliness, or (c) by gradual and imperceptible withdrawal from him—has to search for him in sorrow, with a broken and contrite heart. He must be gentle but earnest in this search. He must seek him not among his relatives and acquaintances but in the Temple in Jerusalem—that is, in the Church, in the sacraments, and in prayer. If we are the persons involved in this, we must abandon our sinful ways, leave behind our worldly ways and our desire to please the world. We must rather desire to please Jesus.[184]

Now, let me only mention some other sufferings or dolors of Mary with Jesus. Consider a mother's pain or anguish at meeting her only son being beaten and made an object scorn and derision by a mob. That was Mary's anguish at meeting Jesus carrying his heavy cross to Calvary and being beaten mercilessly by soldiers and a hostile crowd. And on reaching Calvary, Jesus was stripped naked and nailed to the cross in the presence of his mother. Which mother would not be interiorly shattered by such experience? That was not all; as Mary stood at the foot of the cross and watched her son die in anguish, a soldier pierced the side of Jesus with a lance, and then his dead body was taken down from the cross and given to his mother to carry. And finally, Mary, in great anguish, watched her only son being buried. We can see that Mary suffered much for and with Jesus and deserves honor and devotion not only because she is the mother of Jesus, but also for her coredeeming sufferings that she added to the sufferings of Christ.

Particular Devotions

There are various devotions to our Lady, the Blessed Virgin Mary. But three have been suggested especially for priests, for they have been repeatedly approved by the Church and take up little time. These are the Rosary, the Angelus, and Marian aspirations.

A Marian aspiration or ejaculation is just a raising of the heart to Mary, a call to her for help, an invocation, such as "Jesus mercy, Mary help," or "I am all yours, my mother and my queen," etc. It is not necessary even to pronounce it vocally. It takes no time, and its nature makes it easy to repeat many times during the day. If we remember to perform this regularly, it will become a good habit that will help us to acquire a spirit of prayer.[185]

When we say the Angelus, we give thanks for and recall the beginning of the greatest event that has taken place since the world began, the Christ event. For the Angelus is a prayerful recalling of the Annunciation. We should form the habit of saying it three times in the day: at the end of our morning prayer, at noon, and after our evening prayer. Nothing is wrong, however, if we cannot say it exactly at noon if, for instance, we forget it and remember to say it a little later. Or owing to some difficulty or obstacle, we cannot pray it at exactly 12:00 noon. If possible, we should invite those around us to pray it with us.[186]

The Rosary

The Rosary is perhaps the most characteristic Catholic common prayer. It is Christocentric even though it is Marian in character and, by saying it properly, Christians receive a lot of graces from God through the mother of Jesus. Pope John Paul II notes that "to recite the Rosary is nothing other than to contemplate with Mary the face of Christ."[187] Its importance for the well-being of both individuals and the world is underscored by the fact that our Lady has appeared in several places especially since the nineteenth century, imploring her children to say this prayer. Notable among these appearances are those at Lourdes in France and Fatima in Portugal.[188] Many saints too attest to its effectiveness. Saint Pio of Pietrelcina, for example, despite his tight schedule and the many pilgrims he had to help, recited this prayer many times during each day. Saint Louis-Marie Grignion de Montfort has seen the Rosary as an effective means to convert the most hardened sinners and the most obstinate heretics.[189]

Many popes attach great importance to this prayer. Among them are Pope Pius V, who instituted the feast of the Rosary on October 7, the anniversary of the miraculous victory of Christians over the Turks in 1571, thanks to the public recitation of the Rosary;[190] Pope Leo XIII on September 1, 1883 promulgated his encyclical *Supremi Apostolatus Officio*, in which he proposed the Rosary as "an effective spiritual weapon against the evil forces affecting society." The pope champions of the Rosary since the Second Vatican Council are Blessed John XXIII, Pope Paul VI, and our beloved Pope John Paul II, who always encouraged the saying of the Rosary, pointing out the importance of this Marian prayer in his spiritual life right from his youthful days. On October 29, 1978, at the beginning of his pontificate, he admitted openly and frankly that the Rosary was his favorite prayer. Again, in October 2002, the twenty-fifth year of his pontificate, he gave the Church an important document, his apostolic letter, *Rosarium Virginis Mariae,* which is his reflection on the Rosary.[191]

The Rosary is both a contemplative prayer as well as a vocal prayer—that is, it is both meditation and supplication. I have seen some people, some of them highly placed Christians, who say the Rosary is boring and a mere repetition of *Hail Marys*. This is quite a wrong judgment, a misunderstanding of this widely cherished prayer. It is essentially made of *the Lord's Prayer* and the Angelic Salutation—that is, the *Our Fathers* and *Hail Marys* and then the mysteries of the life of Christ or his mother. As stated above, this prayer is essentially centered on Christ. The succession of *Hail Marys* is an unceasing praise of Christ, who is "the ultimate object" both of the Annunciation and of the greeting of Elizabeth: "Blessed is the fruit of your womb." In other words, in this contemplative/vocal prayer, the *Hail Marys* "constitute the warp on which is woven the contemplation of the mysteries. The Jesus that each *Hail Mary* recalls is the same Jesus whom the succession of mysteries proposes to us now as the Son of God, now as Son of the Virgin."[192]

Before the year 2002, there were three traditional sets of the mysteries of the Rosary, and each set was usually used with five decades of the Rosary. The full Rosary then was fifteen decades. But in that year, Pope John Paul II added a new set of mysteries—that is, the luminous mysteries or the mysteries of light, highlighting the public ministry of Christ. He also modified the order in which the mysteries were arranged for each week and season. Since then, many Christians, including highly placed Catholics, are confused as to what days or seasons to say which of these mysteries. For refreshing of memory, I wish to state the order again here. The new arrangement for the week and seasons is thus: the joyful mysteries are recited on Mondays and Saturdays throughout the year as well as on Sundays in Advent and Christmas season; the luminous mysteries (the mysteries of light) are used on Thursdays throughout the year; the sorrowful mysteries take their turn on Tuesdays and Fridays throughout the year as well as Sundays in Lent; on Wednesdays throughout the year and Sundays outside Christmas season and Lent, it is the glorious mysteries that are said.[193]

Mary is the mother of Jesus and mother of priests. Priests should love her as a good son loves his mother. Among the signs of this love is devotion to her. A good mother she is, and for the priest, she is the best counselor and trusted guide. She understands the difficulties of the priest's work, its dangers, its misunderstandings, and the heroism involved in being human and yet called to mediate between God and men.[194] Happy is the priest who is devoted to her! She should be the priest's refuge in times of sorrow, desolation, and trial. Happy again is the priest who realizes the secret of having Mary as his mother and taking her home as did the Beloved Apostle.

✝

CHAPTER 6

The Trojan Horse in the City of God

Far away and long ago, there was a war. It was between Greece and Troy. It lasted for weeks, months, and then years, and there was no sign of its end. Indeed, it was a long-drawn-out war. Both sides got almost worn out, but neither wished to give up. At last the Greeks thought out a plan that would give them an edge over the enemy. This plan was to build a giant wooden horse with a hollow interior. They filled its interior with their soldiers and gave it to the Trojans ostensibly as an expiatory gift to the Trojan gods. The wooden horse had wheels and was so cleverly constructed that it was not easy to find out that it had either a door or a hollow interior. At night the Greeks wheeled it to the gate of the city of Troy and went back home.

The Trojans woke up the next morning to see the wooden horse at their gate. They knew it was from the enemy, but what was the motive? Nobody could easily answer that question. The Trojans were divided in their opinions on what to do with the seeming gift from the enemy. Some suggested that it be left alone where it was; others wanted it destroyed completely since they feared the Greeks and their gifts. But the more influential citizens were rather convinced that the Greeks, tired of the war, had sent the horse to their gods and had thereby sued for peace. They prevailed on their compatriots to accept the horse and had it wheeled into the city of Troy. The citizens were assured that the war had ended. There was a lot of feasting and rejoicing in Troy in celebration of the apparent end of the war. People relaxed their security awareness and slept soundly at night.

But then that night, while all the Trojans were sleeping, the Greek soldiers inside the horse opened the door and came out. Having distributed themselves to different locations of the city, they set that city on fire. And after raising a war cry, they fled from the city. The Trojans awoke and were thrown into confusion and stampede. In that confusion, they fought and killed one another, for each man thought his neighbor was an enemy soldier. In this way, Troy was defeated and destroyed. This is an epic in Greek mythology.

The foregoing story, however, could be said to be similar to what is happening in the war between the Catholic Church and its enemies. This statement is made in the light of what the Church has been going through since recent years, owing to the relaxation of its security watch. For, from at least the seventeenth to the early twentieth century, the Catholic Church often feared that its enemies, especially communists and secret societies, could smuggle into its seminaries weed among the seeds—that is, men who would later become priests and embarrass or fight the Church from within. With this suspicion in mind, the Church guarded its seminaries and other institutions of formation jealously and was careful in the selection of both seminarians and their formators.

This suspicion was not groundless. For it has indeed been the plan of many of the feared enemies to destabilize and bring down the Church from within. One of these enemies has been the Freemasonry. Since 1738, when Pope Clement XII exposed and condemned this secret society, it has been one of the bitterest enemies of the Church.[195] In the nineteenth century, *Alta Vendita,* the highest lodge of this secret society, sketched a blueprint or plan to destroy the Catholic Church. The name of this blueprint is *The Permanent Instruction of the Alta Vendita.* Since this enemy was aware that it could not harm the Church seriously if it attacked openly, it chose subtle and cunning ways. These include spreading abroad liberal views or ideas and trying to infiltrate into the Church and use the structures of the latter to subvert it.[196] This blueprint is a process that will take decades to accomplish. The architects of the blueprint did not expect to see it completely accomplished in their own lifetime. But they expected it to be accomplished by succeeding generations of their initiated. The plan of this instruction is, first of all, to spread liberal ideas and axioms throughout society and in the institutions of the Church so that lay people, seminarians, priests, and religious would gradually and inadvertently accept liberal ideas and principles. "In time this mind-set would be so pervasive that priests would be ordained, bishops would be consecrated, cardinals would be nominated whose thinking was in step with the modern thought rooted in the French Revolution's Declaration of the Rights of Man."[197] And eventually the Church would elect a liberal pope who, with his liberal hierarchy, would lead the Church on the liberal principles of Freemasonry while at the same time believing they are good Catholics. Rather than oppose modernist ideas and principles, these Catholic leaders would teach them in the Church. The ultimate result would be a church deceptively turned into a cult with most of its members still thinking they are Catholics.[198]

Next, the instruction urges the members of the secret societies to work for success not with adults who have already formed their convictions, but rather through children and youths. They were instructed to infiltrate the Church and pretend to be good Catholics, which will give them the opportunity to plant their seed of deception among the youths and children who would be the hope of the future. The reputation of these enemies as good Catholics would help to sell the doctrine of the secret societies to the young clergy. These in time would hold important assignments or positions in the Church and ultimately elect a pope who would help to implement their modernist or revolutionary principles in the Church. They were confident of ultimate success. For this reason, they were instructed to lay their snares in all the Church's strategic locations: rectories or Fathers' houses, sacristy, seminaries, convents, monasteries, and other important institutions or locations.[199]

The popes of the eighteenth and nineteenth centuries became aware of the dangerous plans of the enemy and fought against them and other hostile trends with their encyclicals, the most devastating of all being Pope Leo XIII's *Humanum Genus* (1884), in which he outlined the aim, methods, and dangers of Freemasonry. The pope states that there are many enemies fighting the Church but that their leader is Freemasonry, whose aim is to destroy the Church and deprive the world of the blessings given to it through Christianity.[200] This secret society does not want only the destruction of the Christian religion, but also of all political systems or governments that have traces of Christianity, and replace them with laws or systems drawn from "Naturalism."[201] The pontiff points out that this secret society undermines all religions, especially the Catholic Church, by teaching its members to be indifferent to all religions and to see them as all alike, without any difference. He warns all to dread and avoid anything to do with Freemasonry.[202] However, despite the efforts of the popes, by the end of the nineteenth century, a new breed of Catholics emerged, some of them clergymen who desired a compromise between the Church's conservative stance and the revolutionary principles of the French Revolution. Thus, the work of the enemy in the Church started successfully and continues to increase.[203]

The crisis started in the nineteenth century had grown big by the beginning of the twentieth in the form of modernism. Pope Saint Pius X, who became pope in 1903, identified liberalism or modernism as a very dangerous plague that must be eradicated. He issued an encyclical, *Pascendi,* and a decree, *Lamentabili,* against this plague, instituted antimodernist oaths to be sworn by priests and theology teachers, removed from seminaries and universities modernists, and excommunicated those who refused to repent. Pope Pius X thus halted the spread of modernism or liberal teachings at his time. But this hydra went underground and resurfaced later in different forms,[204] as we shall see below.

Why Shortage of Priests in the West?

It is strongly believed that the work of the enemy in the Church is playing a devastating role in the crisis that has rocked the Church with its clergy and religious in recent years, especially in North America and Europe. It has harmed the Church in different parts of the world, especially in the formation of the clergy and religious. It is one of the main causes of the shortage of seminarians, the religious, and priests in many places. The shortage of vocations to the priesthood in most parts of North America and Europe has been blamed on a number of factors. These include the failure to instruct the young in the faith, the reluctance of some parents to allow their children to become priests or religious, lifelong celibacy of the priesthood, materialism, skepticism, practical and philosophical atheism, subjectivism, and hedonism. There are others too. An important one that is often overlooked is the fact that some vocation directors and others responsible for promoting vocations are no longer working for the Church but rather working against the Church's interest in seminaries and religious houses. Some seem to be working for the enemies of the Church. Their plan is not to produce priests according to the mind of the Church but rather to reenvision the priesthood according to their own agenda or the agenda of the secret societies that sponsor them or which they pay allegiance to. Hence, they reject candidates who uphold the Church's teaching and accept those who are not suitable.[205]

In other words, the officials entrusted with promoting vocations to the priesthood are the very people destroying them by turning away suitable or qualified candidates for the Catholic priesthood. And the very people who cause artificial shortage of genuine vocations to the priesthood turn round and advocate the ordination of married men and women. There is really no shortage of vocations in dioceses or places where the Catholic Church's teaching about the priesthood is maintained.[206]

A recent research has revealed that various obstacles are intentionally placed in the way of genuine vocations to the priesthood, which lead to the sincere seminarians' early expulsion or voluntary departure, if at all they are admitted into the seminary program. These include a biased process of screening applications; faculty members and spiritual directors who focus on detecting signs of orthodoxy among seminarians in order to make it difficult for them to continue; a practical moral life of some students and faculty that is not compatible with the Christian standard; endorsement of homosexual practices and agenda; promotion of ideas and teachings which undermine Catholic belief in most fundamental doctrines of the Church; open contempt for proper liturgy and traditional devotions; and spiritual and psychological manipulations and abuse.[207]

It is important to note that the situation here is not the procedure designed to eliminate from the seminary those who have no genuine vocations. It is rather a scheme designed to frustrate genuine vocations because the candidates are perceived by those in charge of vocations apparatus as threats to their agenda. For those in positions of authority in many seminaries are motivated by their desire to redesign or rather reenvision the Catholic ministerial priesthood and change Church ministry according to their own model. Their model includes lay-run parishes, secularized worship, women priests, and not taking the Catholic doctrine quite seriously.[208] The suitable candidates or applicants who hold on to the Church's teaching on sex morality are labeled as sexually immature or inflexible. The number of candidates or applicants for priestly training rejected on the grounds that they are orthodox or follow the teaching of the Catholic Church is countless. They were regarded as too traditional, too dogmatic, or too rigid. It was made known to some applicants that the reason they were rejected was their strict allegiance to the pope and their strong devotion to the Virgin Mary.[209] The network is so tight that once a young man with a sincere vocation is expelled from or voluntarily leaves one seminary because of frustration or disgust, they make it extremely difficult for him to be admitted into another seminary. They do this by usually giving undeserved bad reports about him.[210]

There are other ways designed to keep those who have sincere vocations out. In liberal dioceses, the applicants are subjected to a test on their view of what the Church should be. If the applicant admits that he accepts the Church teaching on matters or issues of authority and sexual morality, he is regarded as "rigid" or inflexible and therefore dismissed. One of the most common questions posed to the applicants is about the ordination of women. If the applicant lets them know that he agrees with the stand of the Church on this issue, he is regarded as unfit for modern priesthood and therefore dismissed. Making things worse is the feminization of the apparatus for priestly vocations in places where the male model for priestly vocations is rare. For instance, in some dioceses of North America and Europe, the vocation directors are women. In some others, when a priest is the vocation director, a liberal nun or even a nun who is not in good standing in her religious order is usually the assistant who in fact does much of the work of the director;[211] she has the power to accept or reject an applicant. These nuns or ex-nuns who nourish the hope that one day they will get ordained often reject applicants who hold the Church's position on the ordination of women.[212] What would one expect? Would anyone be surprised if these women disqualified candidates who hold firm to the teaching of the Church on the ordination of women, homosexual activities, priestly celibacy, and use of contraceptives? In a process like this, those who have sincere vocations and who accept the Church's teaching are rejected while liberals and sexual deviants are accepted as candidates for the seminary.[213]

Another trap for eliminating the sincere candidates is the mandatory psychological evaluation of every applicant to the seminary. Sometimes the psychologist may be a man or woman with homosexual or lesbian orientation. He may be a non-Catholic or even a non-Christian. In fact, in some cases, the psychologist may be an open member of a secret society. For instance, the psychologist who was employed by a number of dioceses to evaluate and recommend applicants and candidates for the seminary was the Master of the Washington Masonic Lodge and a member of the Rosicrucian order.[214] Since it was in his power to recommend or reject any applicant to the seminary, he rejected all those who held fast to the Church's teaching or refused to accept the idolatrous and liberal ideas. He rather recommended those who had homosexual orientation and held liberal views. And since 1988, a good number of young priests who were among those candidates recommended by this psychologist and others like him have left the priesthood. Some others have been found guilty of sex abuse. Thus, this Mason and other psychologist members of secret societies are hired to evaluate, recommend, or reject candidates for the Catholic priesthood. Here the psychologists accomplish the plans of their order. They usually screen out the suitable ones and recommend liberals and sexual perverts whose abuses have cost many dioceses many millions of dollars in lawsuits, not to mention the embarrassments and cost to the reputation of the Church in general.[215]

Homosexual Subculture

For those applicants who succeed in being accepted into liberal seminaries, more troubles or problems continue. One of the greatest problems they have to face is homosexual menace. Sincere men who are admitted into homosexual seminaries consider themselves in the wrong place. They feel uncomfortable, out of place, and that they are making a mistake to choose to go to the seminary. How can such people be disposed to study and form themselves as Catholic priests when homosexual activity is practiced openly not only by many seminarians but also a good number of the members of the faculty? The seminarians who refuse to indulge in homosexual activities are seen as the "bad guys," too rigid, and out of tune with the times.[216]

Some seminary authorities no longer hide their homosexual agenda. They confess openly that they admit homosexual men in the seminary or do not inquire about the sexual orientation of applicants before they are admitted. Is it not preposterous or rather unbelievable that a seminary should knowingly make it possible for homosexuals to make up about 70 percent of its student body? And even some of those who were not gay before they entered the seminary have been perverted to join the school of homosexuals. In that case, who would expect strongly heterosexual students to be comfortable and willing to remain in such a seminary?[217] In fact, in some places, some people take it for granted that most priests and seminarians are gay or homosexual. Some have made the conclusion that normal men do not become priests these days.[218] Why should anyone be surprised if vocations to the priesthood fall drastically and many seminaries become empty? This is one of the shocking secrets behind shortage of priests in North America and Europe.[219] Some former homosexual seminarians have been ordained priests and continue to promote their shameful agenda. Some are among those who have caused their dioceses a lot of harm and embarrassment in various ways. One of the homosexual seminaries was Saint John's in Michigan, which was closed by the Vatican in the mid-1980s. There are other seminaries in North America, Europe, and different parts of Africa where the homosexual disease has eaten deep into students and members of the faculty. Where this activity is practiced openly not only by seminarians but also by members of the faculty, who will correct the other or heal the disease? Hope seems to dim for sincere seminarians. How will this problem be overcome?[220]

Members of the faculty and seminarians who are not involved in homosexual activities in these seminaries think they can do nothing to stop them because they are powerless while many of those involved are more powerful and have better connections with those in important positions. For many strong men in the faculty protect and defend gay or homosexual seminarians. Straight men or men not involved in immoral practices are the ones persecuted if they report their ordeals or homosexual advances made by homosexual seminarians or members of the faculty.[221] Those seminarians who accept the Church's teaching on sexual morality are termed homophobes and troublemakers, and some are expelled. Others not expelled are threatened, especially in religious houses, that if they do not submit to the homosexual demands of their fellow seminarians or superiors, their priestly calling would be endangered. The obsession and persecution of sincere men are far worse in religious houses than in diocesan seminaries. In such orders or houses, seminarians who refuse to submit to the homosexual demands of their superiors are expelled on the ground that they are obstinate, difficult to correct or to work with. Before their expulsion, such seminarians are subjected to painful psychological examination for they are considered as unbalanced.[222] Frustrated with the hopeless situation, many good seminarians choose themselves to leave.

Modernist Trends in Seminaries

The problem of sincere seminarians in the liberal seminaries is not immoral activities only. There are also liberal or modernist trends or activities.

These activities, in one way or the other, make it clear that some members of the faculty entrusted with the formation of seminarians do not support the priesthood as the Catholic Church defines it. Nor do they support the Catholic hierarchy, its Eucharist, its liturgy, and its teachings. To make things worse, liberal seminaries admit into their faculty radical feminist nuns who hate the male celibate priesthood and the Church. They maintain that the Church's refusal to acquiesce to their insistent demand for ordination to the priesthood is clear injustice against women. When given the chance, especially the opportunity to teach or form seminarians, they do all they can to subvert the Church from inside. This they do by teaching future priests erroneous and destructive doctrine and contributing to the expulsion of good, sincere, and orthodox seminarians.[223] The aim of these deviant teachers is to teach seminarians that there is no need for them to be priests or to prevent them from becoming good priests. As a result, some seminarians have lost not only their vocation but also their Catholic faith.[224] In addition, secularized theology, such as Rudolf Bultmann's modernist interpretation of the faith in the 1960s, made its way into Catholic seminaries and other institutions of higher learning. This, again, robbed many seminarians of their faith and vocations.[225]

That is not all. Some seminaries seem to admit intentionally as members of their faculties open members of secret societies. These teachers use immoral books with pornographic drawings or pictures to teach seminarians immoral lessons. For instance, a staff psychologist at a seminary in the Northwest of the United States was using as textbook a pornographic book named *Our Sexuality*. When the attention of the seminary authorities was called to this, they were reluctant to withdraw the book and withdrew it only when a seminarian publicly revolted against its continued use.[226]

Now, one of the obvious and often insidious deterrents to the sincere seminarian is heterodoxy or false teaching in the seminary. Several members of faculty are dissident and do not hide their disregard for the Church and its teaching. The seminarian coming into the seminary with the hope of finding the seminary staff or faculty in love with the Church is usually sadly disappointed to find the opposite. Often many of the faculty members use textbooks written by dissidents who hold such divergent ideas as the Bible is not to be taken seriously because of its cultural background, one religion is as good as the other, the pope is not infallible, the Real Presence of Christ in the Eucharist is an antiquated belief; Jesus is not really divine, God is feminine, women should be ordained priests in the name of justice or equality, etc. Some of these ideas have been officially condemned by the Church in its history. For most of them are clearly axioms or ideas of secret societies whose first step in getting converts is usually to create an atmosphere of moral laxity and permissiveness.[227] Some other theories, such as aggressive feminism, taught to seminarians make it clear that those seminary faculties do not have the interest of the Church at heart. A clear example is a religious sister who was allowed to teach in a particular seminary for seventeen years. Her teaching and writings openly show her hatred for the Catholic Church and the male priesthood. Her attitude destroyed many vocations. For many good and sincere seminarians left of their own accord rather than accept false teaching.[228]

Another faculty member of the same seminary denied Christ's institution of two great sacraments without which there can be no Catholic Church, that is, the Eucharist and holy orders. He also denied the sacrificial and atoning nature of Christ's death on the Cross.[229] Such is the rubbish that is taught not only in one or two seminaries but also in good number in North America, Europe, and parts of Africa. The intention of those men and women is not to teach but rather to subvert or undermine the Church from within by destroying the seminary system and converting the young men who intend to be priests to join the company of those who subvert the Church. As a result of this, many seminarians not only lose their vocation and faith but also start hating the Church. But some seminarians who stick to their position of holding the Church's teaching are regarded as rigid and narrow-minded and are usually dismissed. Some others leave on their own since they cannot swallow the false teachings.[230] In these liberal seminaries, the required textbooks are those written by notable dissidents and books aimed at destroying and ridiculing the seminarians' sexual morality.[231]

In one such seminary, the students include both seminarians and lay men and women. Many students were horrified to be in class with a woman who openly advertised herself as a witch, drove around with witch bumper stickers, and had progay symbols on her clothes. Seminarians could do nothing to challenge her because if they did, they would be in trouble. For at that seminary, she was given deference by the members of the faculty. And on the day of her graduation, she attended the ceremony with her friends and posed for several pictures with the rector of the seminary.[232] In some of the seminaries, the formation team includes mainly liberal priests and lesbian women religious, some of whom may have left their order. Their entire effort is to change seminarians to their way of thinking or frustrate out those who cling tenaciously to the Catholic Church's teaching. They have high hopes that not long, considering the shortage of priests, the Catholic Church will begin to ordain women and married men.[233] The litany of the false teachings and bizarre attitudes in many of the seminaries is almost endless—from liberal priests to disgruntled nuns who feel oppressed by the male-dominated Church.

These false teachings and attitudes from seminary staff have their immediate and remote consequences. The immediate result is the erroneous education of the future priests who carry on the erroneous teaching to its remote consequence—that is, teaching the Christian faithful the false teaching, thus perpetuating the errors and weakening the faith and moral of the faithful.[234] They contribute much to the decline of sincere vocations. For many good men are either expelled from the seminary for refusing to embrace the false teachings and attitudes or leave on their own accord disgusted and disenchanted with the Catholic Church.[235] To hasten the destruction of the spiritual life of seminarians, they are denied the opportunity for traditional Catholic devotions such as Eucharistic adoration, benediction of the Blessed Sacrament, public Rosary, and novenas. Serious seminarians are forbidden to say the Rosary anywhere except in their rooms. In many other seminaries in North America and Europe, it is an offence for a seminarian to say the Rosary even in his room. For the formation team claims that praying the Rosary or having any devotion to the Blessed Virgin Mary is an indication of some deficiency in the personality of the seminarian. This boils down to the conclusion that the seminarian is not suitable for the priesthood.[236] If a student bows before Communion, it is counted as an offense because he is obsessed with the Real Presence. Similarly, anyone who kneels after Communion is doing something wrong. Students are forbidden too to kneel down at any part of the Mass, including during the Eucharistic prayer.[237]

In the liturgy itself, there are a lot of abuses. These include the fact that the celebrant often does not use any vestment except a stole, seminarians reading part of the Eucharistic prayer, all standing during the Consecration, use of inclusive language always, Mass being celebrated on a coffee table in priests' rooms, improper matter used for Eucharistic bread and wine, and many other abuses.[238] This may seem unbelievable. But they do really happen even in parishes and other places. Not long ago, for instance, a priest from another country visiting a diocese in the Midwest of the United States was shocked when he was invited for Mass. This so-called Mass was in the living or sitting room of the rectory. What was used as the altar was a bare round coffee table. The pastor of the parish who was the celebrant had no vestments on except a short stole. He and all who attended sat in a circle all through the Mass. For the several days that the visiting priest was there, each Mass lasted about ten minutes, or if the celebrant chose to preach, it lasted for about thirteen minutes. For Communion he would pass round a clay bowl that he used as a ciborium, and each one took his or her Communion as the bowl was passed. Is this not almost a sacrilegious celebration? Who would like to concelebrate or participate in such a Mass? But that is what some parishioners have to face for six years, twelve years, or even a longer period. Why should anyone wonder if some of them lose their faith and either leave the Church or remain there but become impervious to traditional Catholic teaching and practice? Ironically, this pastor was entrusted with the custody of a number of seminarians from East Africa who wished to study and become priests for that diocese; they were sent to this pastor to learn the American culture before they would begin their studies in the seminary. That was their first shock. Is that really the true culture of the American Catholic Church? Such unfaithful men give a wrong impression of the Church in America.

Many seminarians cannot bear or accept these abuses. For instance, a student of a seminary in the Midwest of the United States was warned that he would be penalized if he knelt during Eucharistic consecration or attempted to receive Communion on his tongue. That seminarian chose to leave the seminary the following day. In the same seminary, some female members of the formation staff did not care to attend Mass on weekdays because they saw the all-male celebration as part of the oppression of women.[239] And one may ask here why at all women should be part of the formation staff of a seminary. Much of the formation is to provide the role model of the male priesthood. How can women provide this? Just as it would be wrong for men to be formators of women aspiring to be women religious, so also it is wrong for women to be formators of candidates for the Catholic priesthood. Women could be employed as classroom teachers in the seminary, if need be, but not as formators of seminarians.

Even in some seminaries, attending Mass on weekdays is optional; and in some still, there are no Masses on weekdays. Rather than celebrate Mass on weekdays, some of these seminaries celebrate what they call quasiliturgies, some of which include popular feminist themes and new age themes that are clearly opposed to Christianity. Even though those celebrations are a mockery of the Mass, faculty members promote and use them.[240]

Psychological Counseling as Trap

The problems faced by good men in liberal seminaries are enormous and daunting. These include gay subculture, radical feminism, spiritual misdirection, false teaching, political correctness, bad liturgy, and lack of spirituality. All these have their effects on the seminarian who has come to prepare himself for the Catholic priesthood. Being human, seminarians are affected by their environment—and in this case, a hostile one. Some priests who managed to pass through the system compare what the seminarian goes through to the brainwashing of the communist reeducation camps—that is, the seminarian is subjected to give up all the right knowledge and upright behavior that he had before and adopt the wrong and sinful ones proposed by the seminary formation team. If he opposes the teaching or wrongdoings, he is regarded as mentally unfit and kept under close scrutiny. Almost all the methods of the communist system of the former USSR were employed in many seminaries in America, especially in 1980s and 1990s. Even fellow seminarians spied on one another. There were slander, intimidations, threats, blackmail, and other evil means to maintain the sinful situation.[241]

Thus, in liberal seminaries, the formation team uses every aspect of intimidation techniques to make the good seminarian uncomfortable so that he may choose to leave on his own volition. If he fails to go, they usually find a way to incite him to rebel against the system. Then this gives the team the desired opportunity to label him obstinate or belligerent and therefore unfit for ordination. One of the most common intimidation techniques was the application of psychological counseling. Sincere seminarians were sent for ongoing psychological counseling for their Catholic faith. Seminarians who failed to take seriously these sessions, which usually tried to brainwash them to give up their Catholic beliefs, were expelled.[242]

The psychological counseling was designed to achieve two results. The first was to make the seminarian begin to doubt that he had a vocation to the priesthood; and to those who did not yet have a strong vocation, those who were yet trying to discern their vocation, it gave the excuse or rather occasion to make the decision that they had no vocation to the priesthood. The other aim for the counseling was to brainwash the sincere seminarian to change to liberal beliefs. If he continued to remain adamant, he was expelled. It is now clear that in a good number of seminaries in the United States, many seminarians were expelled for their faith and upright living.[243]

The numerous reports about the destruction of vocations through perverted psychological evaluation and counseling led the Catholic Medical Association to form a task force made up of eight physicians, four of whom were also psychiatrists, a professional psychologist, and a moral theologian to evaluate the situation. After the group's findings, the association in 1999 made a position statement that frowned at the practice of choosing "mental health professionals" who did not support the Catholic Church's teaching on sexuality to "evaluate the candidates for the priesthood and reject candidates that do accept the Church's teaching on the grounds that they are 'rigid.'" It also frowned at the purposeful customary failure of the mental health practitioners to report homosexual orientations and conflicts in candidates for the priesthood to diocesan officials or religious superiors. The association then made some recommendations to church authorities: "Unless there are signs of severe breakdown, there should be no need to retest a person who has been evaluated within the next five years" for "the basic personality structure does not change." It made it clear to the seminary authorities that "adherence to the teaching of the Catholic Church on sexuality and particularly on homosexuality is not a sign of mental illness, but mental health." It further recommended that no seminarian should be referred for retesting because he supports the teaching of the Catholic Church and none of them should be retested unless he "shows clinically significant evidence of serious mental disorder." The medical association rejected referring candidates for the Catholic priesthood to non-Catholic psychologists or even to Catholics who did not support the Church's teaching. It generously offered to help bishops and religious superiors in this task by preparing a list of qualified mental health practitioners who would be suitable for evaluating these candidates.[244]

We can see now that priest shortage in the West in most cases is man-made, artificial; it was mainly caused by those entrusted with promoting priestly vocations who turn away suitable candidates because they support or accept the teaching of the magisterium. It is the same people who predict that there will be greater shortage of priests in future. They therefore proffer their solution: remove priestly celibacy and recall priests who have already abandoned the priesthood. In addition, they advocate the ordination of women. Feminist groups on their part see the reservation of the priesthood to the celibate men alone as the last trace of the discrimination against women and hope that this dispensation will collapse to make way for the ordination of women. The advocates of the ordination of women and of scraping celibacy from the priesthood have a good number of supporters. It is surprising to note that among those supporters are some diocesan bishops in North America who see the shortage of priests in their land as a sign of the Holy Spirit telling them to ordain married men.

They blame the shortage and cases of sex-abuse scandal on celibacy imposed on the priesthood.[245]

But they also should ask why, in some parts of the world or even some dioceses of the United States, there are increases in priestly vocations despite the discipline of celibacy. Such dioceses as Lincoln, Bridgeport, Omaha, Arlington, Peoria, Wichita, Atlanta, and Rockford are examples of dioceses in the United States where increases in vocations to the priesthood are steady every year. We have adequately pointed out one of the causes of priestly shortage and clergy sex-abuse cases. It is the fact that those entrusted with the promotion of vocations to the male celibate priesthood have a death wish for this age-old brand of the priesthood. They therefore dismiss or frustrate out of the seminary candidates who would be good priests. They rather choose liberal and homosexual men to promote their own agenda and thus undermine the Catholic Church's intention and scheme.

What Is the Cause of the "Earthquake"?

The crisis in the priesthood and the Church in some parts of the world nowadays is dealing a serious blow on the mystical body of Christ. This blow could be compared to an earthquake. What is the ultimate cause? We have already seen a number of proximate causes, especially the fact that people entrusted with the promotion of vocations are intentionally and systematically frustrating or rejecting suitable candidates and accepting unsuitable ones. But how did these wrong people occupy these important positions, and why is their presence so pervasive? This leads us back to the title of this chapter and our position in the first part of the chapter that the Trojan horse has been smuggled into the city of God: enemies of the Church have successfully infiltrated into its ranks and file to see to the successful carrying out of the plan of the Freemasonry, other secret societies, and other enemies of the Church—to undermine the Church, to subvert it from within. It is important to take note of this statement.

In the 1920s and 1930s, an elite clique of homosexual Marxists called the Cambridge Apostles were very powerful. This group under the leadership of Anthony Blunt was determined to take control of all the major institutions, especially the churches, the mass media, the cinema, the universities, the museums, and the government cultural agencies. It has been discovered how Blunt placed his friends, both Marxists and homosexuals, in some of the most important cultural agencies in the western world. Furthermore, some of the former Communists in the United States have confessed that, in the 1930s, more than a thousand communists were encouraged to enter Catholic seminaries. One of them, Bella Dodd, testified: "In the 1930s, we put eleven hundred men into the priesthood in order to destroy the Church from within."[246]

This discovery (which corroborates our earlier assertions) explains some of the seeming riddles in the scandal in the church in North America and Europe. One widely respected but now deceased prelate, probably a product of this clique, used its method in creating a network of gay or homosexual men and pedophiles whose legacies are rocking the Church today. This prelate, who was a dissenter at heart, aided and empowered dissenters while he hypocritically professed his loyalty to Rome. He was the brain behind the proposals to deconstruct the Catholic Church's liturgy, education, and especially religious education or catechetics, especially in the United States. With his exalted position in his country, he influenced the selection of bishops (some of whom are still in power) who would condone and promote pedophilia and homosexual lifestyle in the church. These men and their group have made far-reaching contributions to causing and escalating sex-abuse scandals and other confusions in the church in North America.[247]

We can see further how the infiltration or rather inroad of enemies into the priesthood and other Catholic Church's institutions was masterminded and executed by two of its greatest enemies, namely Marxist communists and Freemasonry. Despite the Church's condemnations of Freemasonry in the 1950s and especially the 1960s, a magazine and some priests started campaigning for the Church's reconciliation with this secret society. At first their effort seemed fruitless. But they continued, arguing that the American Masonry, unlike the Scottish Rite Masonry, was reformed, progressive, and not hostile to the Church. Their persistence gradually started to yield the desired result, for they eventually won the sympathy of some American bishops who probably misunderstood the Second Vatican Council's stand on non-Christians. In 1965, at the Scottish Rite temple in South Bend, Indiana, a bishop addressed a group of Masons and had friendly interactions with them. Later, some other bishops started speaking at Masonic gatherings.[248] On March 5, 1981, another bishop was presented with the Grand Master Award by Rhode Island's Grand Lodge of Masonry. For this bishop was permitting some Catholics in his diocese to join the Masons.[249] This open friendship between these highly placed churchmen and the Freemasonry plus the outright permission of some bishops to Catholics to join the Masons seemingly absolved that secret society of all the condemnations of several popes. Hence, a good number of Catholics in the United States, including some future seminarians and priests, saw nothing wrong in joining the Freemasonry. But on November 26, 1983, the Holy Office or the Sacred Congregation for the Doctrine of the Faith, headed by then Cardinal Joseph Ratzinger (now Pope Benedict XVI), issued a fresh document confirming the Catholic Church's centuries-old position on Freemasonry. It states that this secret society is irreconcilable with the Catholic doctrine. It reminds Catholics that membership in Freemasonry automatically excludes them from Holy Communion. Here is the statement called "Declaration on Masonic Associations."

> It has been asked whether there has been any change in
> the Church's decision in regard to Masonic associations
> since the new Code of Canon Law does not mention them
> expressly, unlike the previous Code

This Sacred Congregation is in a position to reply that this circumstance is due to an editorial criterion which was followed also in the case of other associations likewise unmentioned inasmuch as they are contained in wider categories.

Therefore the Church's negative judgement in regard to Masonic association remains unchanged since their principles have always been considered irreconcilable with the doctrine of the Church and therefore membership in them remains forbidden. The faithful who enroll in Masonic associations are in a state of grave sin and may not receive Holy Communion.

It is not within the competence of local ecclesiastical authorities to give judgment on the nature of Masonic associations which would imply a derogation from what has been decided above, and this in line with the Declaration of this Sacred Congregation issued in February 1981.[250]

Before this document was issued, however, many Catholics in America had joined the Freemasonry, so it was easy for its members to be in positions of importance in the Catholic Church there. Hence, it was not difficult for them to introduce subversive schemes into Catholic institutions. They applied a number of subtle means to bring this about. One of the ways their plan was planted in the Church and succeeded in turning even the Church's children into enemies was by way of a movement or program called the Human Potential Movement, which became popular in the United States and parts of Europe in the late 1960s and 1970s.[251] This movement is simply "a religion of the self." The program or movement that used sensitivity training of encounter groups was wholeheartedly embraced at this period by many heads of Catholic institutions. Vocations directors and heads of seminaries, monasteries, convents, and other Catholic institutions in Europe and North America, especially the United States, quickly adopted it in their institutions. Those in charge of Catholic educational and formation institutions, especially seminaries and novitiates, were made to believe that the movement or program would help them to make deeper contact with the students and thus make them better Catholics. But they were deceived. For the movement replaced the traditional self-sacrifice model of the priesthood and religious life with the self-fulfillment model. And not long after, the program made both the Catholic educators and those they tried to educate liberals and non-Catholics. Many lost their faith. Most of the priests and religious brothers and sisters who utilized the program dropped out of the priesthood and religious life. But before they left, they had sown the seed of the program in the system. They passed their philosophy and devastating psychology to their students, some of whom still have important positions of authority in the Church and society.[252]

The Human Potential Movement or program sees all rules in institutions as a sort of oppression and therefore renders them invalid. This is in agreement with the tenets of Freemasonry, which sees discipline as oppression.[253] The rules that were the protective framework in these institutions—that is, the framework that prevented undue intimacy—were set aside. The consequence was that everybody was silently declared free to do what he liked, to perform an impure act or do any other thing. Or if one is not inclined to do that, to sympathize with those who do. This means it introduced corruption and permissiveness in those institutions beginning from the top down.[254] It sowed the seed of liberalism in the Church or aggravated the growth of liberalism in different countries. It has destroyed many Catholic seminaries and other institutions—for instance, Saint Anthony's Seminary at Santa Barbara, California. It is largely responsible for the sex-abuse crisis. An expert in humanistic psychology has observed that it is not celibacy that drives some priests and religious to pedophilia and other sexual perversions but bad philosophy or some illness contracted by getting involved with bad psychology such as the Human Potentials Movement, which sets aside celibacy and the framework that helps celibacy. Celibacy, he said, is not the cause of the sex-abuse scandal; it is rather loss of faith and prayer life.[255]

Furthermore, some seminaries and dioceses seem to aid this loss of faith and prayer life. Instead of teaching seminarians the traditional spirituality that produced saints in the Church, they send them to sex workshops, show them pornographic videos, and even use scandalous books for the sex education of these young minds. They do this under the pretext of giving the seminarians mature sex education. Is it not rather a subtle or even a clear way of discouraging celibacy and destroying vocations?[256] Prudent and God-fearing men and women are very careful about what should be done or avoided in the sex education of young adults and teenagers. A holy pope advising Catholics on sex-education warns, "It is . . . very important that the prudent father, when speaking to his son on this delicate subject, should be extremely careful and not describe in detail the various ways in which this infernal hydra infects so great a part of the world with its poison."[257] Are these dioceses and seminaries acting as good and prudent fathers by exposing young minds to sex workshops and pornographic videos or films? They also perform other bizarre actions that surely destroy vocations to the priesthood. For instance, a diocesan bishop, not long after he came to power, went as far as closing a formerly thriving seminary and sent the seminarians to a coeducation college. From there, almost all of them lost their desire for the priesthood. This bishop did this without any good reason. A fellow bishop from another diocese had implored him not to close the seminary and sent him a blank check should the cause of his move be financial costs. Despite this godly act from his brother bishop, he carried out his intention. Why? Because he thought he had too many priests.[258]

There is another group of men and women, even highly placed churchmen, who see the scarcity of priests as ushering in a revolution and the death of the present structure of the Church. This is the group that thinks we have arrived at the era of the laity. The group is made up of those who have been advocating the clericalization of the laity and laicization of the clergy. It prefers the service of the laity to that of the clergy in the Church. In some places, it is already in operation. For instance, in some parishes, at a Mass in which several priests are concelebrating, the pastor who is always the chief celebrant prefers that the laity help as ministers of Communion while the concelebrating priests sit down and watch. Indeed, in some places, some bishops and those under them seem to rejoice over the decreasing number of vocations to the priesthood. They see it as an opportunity for creating or evolving a new structure of the Church in which the laity are in charge in most affairs of their church or diocese. In some of these places, arrangements have been made for lay people and nuns to be heads or administrators of parishes while priests are contracted to say Mass and, where need be, to celebrate the other sacraments. Other pastoral ministry or services are done by the laity.[259]

It is obvious that in places where lay ministry is emphasized, the priestly vocation/ministry is devalued and loses attraction for young men who need challenges. The emphasizing of the lay ministry in North America and Europe is one of the subtle ways of discouraging vocations to the priesthood. Are those who do this not compounding rather than solving the problem of priest shortage? This point was stressed by Pope Benedict XVI on May 11, 2006, in his address to Canadian bishops who were on their *ad limina* visit. The pontiff, while appreciative of the services of the laity in the Church, however, warns that their services must never obscure "the absolutely irreplaceable ministry of priests in the life of the Church." Priestly ministry, he said, cannot be entrusted to "others without effectively prejudicing the very authenticity of the Church's being." He wondered how young men would want to become priests if the role of the ordained ministry is not clearly defined and recognized.[260]

As can be carefully observed, all that has been happening to the Church and the current shortage of priests in the West are not simply an aggregate of unrelated facts or evil actions. But they are rather intimately connected. They in fact sprang up from a massive, concerted movement to destroy all traces of traditional Catholicism and replace it with a pseudoreligion, a religion that destroys man's relation with God but which would be appealing to homosexuals, pedophiles, and others like them—a church where people would be free to do what they like. In a word, they want to turn the Church into a cult! Is this not the work of the enemy, the craft of secret societies? This movement wants a new and modern Catholic Church. Unfortunately, some are working for the enemy without knowing it. Or are they too members of the underground movement? Otherwise, how could anyone explain why some bishops are involved in this—bishops who are in full communion with the pope and should work in complete concert with him? And how else can anyone explain why a bishop is liberal or has liberal tendencies? And still more, how else can anyone understand why the ordinary of a diocese, when confronted with the issue of his diocese employing a psychologist openly known as a member of the Freemasonry to screen and recommend aspirants to the priesthood, simply cited the psychologist's academic qualifications.[261] The movement is largely responsible for the sex-abuse scandal that rocked the Church in the United States, especially in the year 2002.[262] Priests and religious involved were in hundreds. Their actions brought a lot of sorrow to Pope John Paul II and many other Catholics. Addressing American cardinals and bishops who came to inform him of the ugly situation in their country on April 24, 2002, the pope expressed sadness at the actions of some priests and religious and the way some bishops are perceived to have handled the scandals: these have made the Church to be viewed with distrust. He viewed the sex scandals as wrong, sinful, and even criminal and sympathized with the victims and their families. He made it clear that there is no place in the Church for priests and religious who abuse the young or who live immoral lives. The pontiff noted that the abuse of the young is a symptom of an illness that has affected not only the Church but also the society as a whole.

However, the Church sometimes seems to be helpless in combating this esoteric movement that has grown very powerful especially in the West, where homosexual priests and religious have formed a very strong clique or rather network for the welfare of the movement. This network protects their members from church discipline or prosecution and makes every effort to see that homosexuals have institutional power in the Church. Some members have important positions in the Church, such as the chancery or seminary management. Many orthodox bishops have been misled by cliques or networks of this nature to include in the religious education of their schools bizarre sex-education programs that not only give to mere children graphic information about normal sexual acts but also brainwash them from a very early age to believe that homosexuality is superior to heterosexuality. The desire of some members of the clergy to dissent, the proliferation of occult and New Age ideas and movements, as well as the atheistic study of Jungian psychology have worked powerfully together to create a picture of a group of men and women who are not Christians but who have, for many years, hijacked the Church with the aim of turning it into a cult.[263]

As it is, the sex scandal that broke open in the United States in 2002 is only the tip of the iceberg. There are a lot of abuses in doctrine, liturgy, and other ways. These abuses affect all Catholics in one way or another, for the Church is like a family or a body. An injury of a member of the body or family is shared by other members. For instance, the sex scandals in the United States caused shame and sadness not only to Catholic priests everywhere but also to all Catholics. This view was articulated by Pope John Paul II at the World Youth Day in Toronto, Canada, in 2002. In his homily at the concluding Mass of the rally on Sunday, July 28, the pope called the sex scandals of priests and religious a source of shame for Catholics. He stated, "The harm done by some priests and religious to the young and vulnerable fills us all with a deep sense of sadness and shame." He counseled especially young Catholics not to be discouraged but to love the Church if they loved Jesus. He admonished them to be consoled by the fact that there were very many priests and religious who were faithful to their vocations and loyal to the Church. These they were to take as models and guides. And he added, "But think of the vast majority of dedicated and generous priests and religious whose only wish is to serve and to do good."[264]

In addition to the shame and sadness caused by the immoral and other deviant actions, the Catholic Church has been made an object of scorn and ridicule before the world, owing to these actions. Files and documents that were formerly regarded as confidential in chanceries and rectories are now laid bare for scrutiny by legal experts and law-enforcement agents who are intent on fishing out old cases of clerical immorality that were not given proper attention. While the official Church has thus been forced to undergo much humiliation because of the actions of these unfaithful men and women that it once called its own and entrusted with a lot of responsibilities, some of the perpetrators are not perturbed.

Through warped preaching and other ways, priests in the movement who are still working in the Church make every effort to confuse and mislead the faithful. Is it not, for instance, a calculated ploy to mislead or confuse the parishioners if the pastor openly tells his congregation (or puts in the parish bulletin) his doubts about the certainty of the Church's feasts of Easter, Ascension, Pentecost, Assumption, and others, or when he tells them not to seek a saint's intercession? Many have virtually trained almost all their parishioners to stop going to confession either by persistently celebrating only general absolution or by telling those who request for individual confession that there is no need to receive that sacrament often. There are many other ways by which the faith of Catholics is disturbed or weakened.[265]

But the crisis is not limited to North America and Europe; it extends also to the so called third world countries, though the magnitude may not be the same. The problem of some priests in these areas seems to be loss of focus. Some seem to have crisis of identity and endeavor to compensate for what they regard as their loss with materialist tendencies. Especially many young ones hate anyone in authority whom they cannot manipulate or deceive easily. Seminary authorities, especially in places where the enemies of the Church have not totally hijacked the apparatus for priestly and religious formation, must be careful not only in the manner they recruit seminarians but also their teachers or formators. The seminaries and novitiates themselves must be made conducive places for priestly formation. Both the Second Vatican Council and Pope John Paul II's postsynodal apostolic exhortation, *Pastores Dabo Vobis*, see the need for these conditions.[266] This time the introduction of antimodernist or antiliberal oaths for formators in seminaries, novitiates, and other Church institutions will not be out of place. These oaths helped Pope Saint Pius X to combat or overcome Modernists in early twentieth century. And not long ago, a bishop who took over in a diocese saw that many people were out of tune with the teaching and practice of traditional Catholicism. He compiled a number of statements that he called *The Affirmation of Faith*. He made it obligatory for anyone in the diocese working or performing any action on behalf of the Church such as those who teach religious education, ushers, and readers at Mass to declare before their bishop or pastor to follow those guidelines. This made a big difference since many who did not wish to affirm to these declarations either by themselves discontinued their function or they were stopped by the church. A lot of things became normal after this.[267]

Again, these formators and bishops must take every step to see that the trends or actions that are dealing ruinous blows in many seminaries and other church institutions are wiped out of their institutions. Such are, for instance, homosexuality, lesbianism, moral laxity or permissiveness, and the like. There are already rumors of either a few cases or large-scale practice of homosexuality and immoral activities in some seminaries in the third world. Such trends no doubt destroy seminaries and other institutions. To play the ostrich and think that such evils will go by themselves is mere wishful thinking and self-deception; it is a disservice to the Church and society.

Moreover, we should not deceive ourselves with the thought that the secret societies have stopped sending their members into the Church institutions. Careful men and women in places of formation know that this is still happening, especially in places where vocations seem to be booming. Seminary authorities and others who are part of the formation apparatus in all institutions of formation who do not have this at the back of their minds may, through inadvertence, make the Church pay dearly still in future. Secret societies, not necessarily Freemasonry (or those cults or societies whose hallmark is violence) have never stopped making serious efforts to send their members, both male and female, into the Church institutions. Careful formators know this quite well for they have come face-to-face with the reality. Everyone who loves the Church must know that there is a war between good and evil, between light and darkness, and must enlist on the side of light.

Afterword

God loves all human beings and wants them to be saved and come to the knowledge of the truth.[268] For this purpose, he sent his only begotten Son, Jesus Christ, into the world. He became man and lived among human beings. By his life, death, and resurrection, Jesus liberated the world from the shackles of evil and sin. Before going back to God the Father, Jesus Christ founded the Church, which is his mystical body or the prolongation of his historical presence in the world. To this Church he transferred the mission given to him by God the Father—the mission to save the world. The Church has been involved in this mission for two thousand years, thanks especially to its priesthood instituted for it by its founder and head Jesus Christ.

But since recent decades, there have been continuous crises in the Catholic priesthood. What are the causes of these crises? Many people have given their opinions. But in this book, efforts have been made to show that these crises were created essentially by the enemies of the Church with the cooperation of some of those the Church once called its own. It is clear to us that not all men believe in God. Some of these non-believers have equated their atheism with their adventure to achieve man's mental and personal liberation from the tyranny of a God "who imposed upon mankind from above the shackles of crystalloid creeds and moral dictates." These atheists claim to be interested in liberating man from these shackles by dissolving what they regard as the religious myth that was forced upon him during the darkness of his infantile ignorance.[269] Especially Marxism, Freemasonry, and other secret societies wish to destroy all religions, particularly the Catholic Church, which is the greatest force against evil in the world. But they found the Church too strong for them for an open and frontal battle.

However, they were quite wise to realize the indispensable role and place of priests in the Church. Convinced that if they succeeded in disturbing the Catholic priesthood, they would have big success in their attempt to disturb the whole Church, they started early trying to infiltrate into the formation institutions for the Catholic priesthood—namely, the seminaries and novitiates. A good number of them succeeded in becoming priests and have embarked upon their plan of fighting the Church from within.

They are responsible directly or indirectly for most of the sex-abuse cases in North America and Europe. They are directly responsible in that, in a few of the cases, they themselves are the perpetrators. But a larger number of the cases originate from them indirectly. For a good number of them having infiltrated the Church formed a large network that helped to see their members in key positions in the Church, especially in the so-called developed countries. Some of them became formators in seminaries and novitiates. Here they made (and in some places are still making) serious efforts to prevent suitable candidates from becoming priests while intentionally admitting and protecting those they were sure were unsuitable. Many of these unsuitable candidates have been ordained priests and are largely those who are causing the Church the pains and embarrassment it has been experiencing in recent years.

While the enemies who have been smuggled into the Church are fighting from within, their counterparts outside the Church play their own role from their external locations. Apart from those mentioned before, there are a few other enemies. Probably the greatest of these other external enemies are some of the secular social media. These media (many of them owned or run by atheistic, greedy, and corrupt individuals or corporations who consider the Church an enemy because of its stand against irreligion, corporate greed, selfishness, pornography, and immorality in general, which they thrive in) wish always to present the Church in a bad light in order to render it less credible to the public. For a long time, they have fought the Church even without provocation and have caused a lot of confusion and damage to this institution. In recent or rather modern times, especially from the beginning of the Second Vatican Council, some of the secular media's hostility to the Catholic Church has remained unabated. That council was convoked for a total renewal of the whole Church. Unfortunately, the media gave the interpretation that by renewal, the Church meant lowering its moral standards and watering down its doctrines. While the council was going on, these media were giving the masses wrong information and interpretations of the council's decisions. By the time the council ended, they had already biased the minds of many Catholics, particularly in the West, or worked up their minds to expect a relaxation of the Church's teaching especially on sexual morality. When the council's teachings, however, did not agree with what the secular social media had promised, many people were disappointed and a good number rebelled against the Church. Many lay people left the Church. This contributed also to a good number of priests and religious abandoning their vocations.

The media and entertainment industry have continued their unmitigated attacks on the Church and its hierarchy. Have they not attacked even the sex morality of Jesus himself? If the media have the guts to do such to Jesus Christ himself, who should be surprised when they attack his followers?[270] Without good reason, they have continued to attack our popes, faithful or orthodox bishops, and priests of the Catholic Church. Especially since their propaganda to make the Church relax its moral teaching failed, they mounted their groundless attacks on Popes John Paul II and Benedict XVI. Every sincere human being in the world, whether Catholic or not, thanked God for the gift of the saintly and charismatic Pope John Paul II. But instead of praising God for the pope's contribution toward peace, brotherly love, and progress in the world, the western media in the last years of the pope found fault with him in one way or another. For a long time, they insinuated the idea that he was too old and sick to continue as pope, thinking they could influence either the pope himself or the Church as a whole for his resignation. But seeing that their efforts were not paying off, their comments about him often became negative.

An example may be the pope's visit to the Americas between July 23 and August 1, 2002. While he was in Toronto, Canada, for the World Youth Day, instead of praising the efforts the aged and sick pope was making to overcome the odds against him and to bolster the faith of the world's young people, the secular social media concentrated their comments on the pope's physical frailty and the way he pronounced the words. Only after his first day there, they were complaining loudly that he had not condemned publicly the clerical sex scandals in America, as if he came to Canada simply to condemn the scandal. And then at the closing Mass of the rally, when he voiced out his condemnation of the scandals, they were happy and repeated it many times in the televisions, radios, and newspapers. And while he was in Mexico for the canonization of Juan Diego, the first indigenous saint of the Americas, they tried to raise doubts as to the historicity of an individual called Juan Diego. Did he ever exist? they questioned. Some of them were of the opinion that if he ever existed, he did not deserve to be canonized. The pope was making the canonization, they opined, simply to retain Latin American Catholics who were leaving the Catholic Church in big numbers. As to the number of people that attended the ceremony, the media reported hundreds of thousands, while in fact it was estimated that about twelve million people (including Vicente Fox, the president of Mexico by that time) were present.

And since Pope Benedict XVI has come to the throne of Peter, the secular social media have continued to present him in a negative light. The clergy sex-abuse cases have supplied them new ammunition. They have especially tried to link the pope with sex-abuse cases he knew nothing about. Most Catholic priests regret the fact that a few priests, including a number of bishops, have been involved in sex abuse cases. They also sympathize with the victims of the abuses. The secular media, however, seems bent on painting every Catholic priest (or the whole Church) as a sex offender. These attacks have irritated even some non-Catholics. Writing in a diocesan monthly journal recently, an elderly Jewish gentleman states, "During my entire life I've never seen a greater vindictive, more scurrilous, biased campaign against the Catholic Church as I have seen in the last 18 months."[271] It should not be any surprise to an intelligent observer that the secular media, which are quite determined to pull the Church's name to the dust, are in fact in the same hostile camp as some of the erring priests. While these priests fight from inside, their counterparts in the social media spread and often exaggerate their actions to tarnish the image of the Church. Faithful Catholics should therefore be careful and sieve the information they receive in the social media these days. A lot of them are false and misleading.

But how is the Church to prevent the recurrence of embarrassments from priests in future? A lot of efforts have been made already. A few examples can be mentioned here. The Second Vatican Council issued two documents—one for the formation of future priests, *Optatam Totuis,* and the other for the life and ministry of priests, *Presbyterorum Ordinis.* On March 25, 1992, Pope John Paul II issued his rather bulky postsynodal apostolic exhortation "on the Formation of Priests in the Circumstances of the Present Day" termed *Pastores Dabo Vobis (I Will Give You Shepherds).* Two years later, the Congregation for Clergy published the *Directory on the Ministry and Life of Priests.* In addition to all these, Pope John II on every Holy Thursday from 1979 to 2004 sent letters to all the Catholic priests in the world, each of these letters dealing with one aspect of the priesthood (or priestly life) or another. Despite these efforts and others, there are obviously a lot of problems.

A few more suggestions can be made here, especially for the places of formation.

- The formation teams in some of the seminaries are to be overhauled, following the guidelines of *Optatam Totius* and *Pastores Dabo Vobis.* And the Church should be more careful in selecting suitable priests for the formation. Academic qualifications alone are not enough for a priest to be a member of the staff of a seminary or novitiate.

- Antimodernist or antiliberal oaths for formators should be reintroduced in seminaries and other institutions of formation.

- Large seminaries should be decongested. No seminary of philosophy or theology should have more than 250 students on campus at the same time. This helps for better formation. Quality is not to be sacrificed on the altar of large numbers. More seminaries could be built so that the decongestion does not deny sincere candidates the opportunity to study for the priesthood.

- The staff should be careful and sincere in selecting candidates for formation and forming them according to the mind of the Catholic Church. Unsuitable candidates should be detected in time and directed to another calling in life other than the priesthood. All forms of stubbornness, indiscipline, moral laxity, especially homosexuality, should be treated as enemies not only of the institution but also of the Church as a whole. Formators should be made to know how delicate and all-important this undertaking is and must resolve never to disappoint God and his Church.

Notes

1   Psalm 65:4

2   Acts 4:12.

3   John 14:6

4   Hebrews 9:12

5   Hebrews 7:24-25

6   Acts 9:1 ff

7   See I Corinthians 12, Vatican, II, L.G. # 1

8   John 20:21

9   In Amala clan, the traditional ruler of the town had the prefix *ezeala* before his name. Though he was called the ruler, he hardly made any important decision about the town without consulting and discussing it with elders.

10 *Ndi nwanwa, ndi odie, ndi nwadiala*, etc. mean the same thing, depending on the locality. Each of the terms means "the sons of our daughters."

11 Cf. Nicene Creed.

12 Pope John Paul II, *Tertio Millennio Adveniente*, (1994) #4. Cf. also Acts 4:12; 1 Tim. 2:5.

13 Pope John Paul II, Letter To Priests, Holy Thursday 2000 #7.

14 John Paul II, *Tertio Millennio Adveniente* (1994) #6

15 Idem Letter to Priests 2000. #8

16 Heb. 8:1-2.

17 Pope John Paul II, Letter to Priests, Holy Thursday 2000 #7.

18 Jn. 1:51; cf. Gen 28:12.

19 Jn. 14:6.

20 Heb. 7:24-25.

21 Cf. 1Sam 15:22; Proverbs. 21:27;Ps. 40:7ff; 50:16-23; Sirach 34:18ff.

22 Cf. Is. 1:11-16; Am. 4:4-5; Sirach 35:11f.

[23] 13 Cf. Ps. 51:18f.

[24] Sirach 35:1-10; Dan. 3:38ff.

[25] Charles Hauret, "Sacrifice" in *The Theology of Atonement* ed. John R. Sheets (Eaglewood Cliffs, New Jersey: Prentice Hall Inc. 1967), pp. 119 ff.

[26] Jn. 10:17-18.

[27] Jesus, the Lamb of God, was the only one who could break the scroll sealed with seven seals—i.e., he was the only one who knew, revealed, and carried out God's secret plan of salvation. See Revelations 5:1-10.

[28] Jn. 10:17

[29] Rom. 5:18-19.

[30] Philip. 2:5-8.

[31] Rom. 5:1-11.

[32] Cf. Lk. 22:42.

[33] Cf. Philippians 2:6-11.

[34] Schmaus, *DOGMA*: vol. 5, *The Church as Sacrament* (Kansas City and London: Sheed and Ward, 1975) pp. 80-81; Paul de Surgy, *The Mystery of Salvation Step by Step through the Bible* (London: Sheed and Ward, 1978), p. 159.

[35] Cf. Heb. 10:6-10; psalm 40:6-8.

[36] Mk. 10:45; cf. Isaiah 53:10ff.

[37] Mt.26:2; Jn. 11:55ff; 12:1; 13:1

[38] Mt. 26:28f; Mk. 14:24f.

[39] Cf. Dt. 12:18; 14:26.

[40] Schmaus, op. cit. pp. 122ff. cf. Heb. 9:12-14

[41] Vatican II, *Constitution on the Church* (*Lumen Gentium*, hereinafter *Lumen Gentium* or LG), #10.

[42] Sacred Congregation for the Clergy, *Directory for the Ministry and Life of Priests* (hereinafter SCC, Directory), 1994, #1.

[43] Pope John Paul II, Novo Incipiente Nostro, "Letter to Priests, April 6, 1979, #3.b.

[44] Synod of Bishops, "The Ministerial Priesthood," Ultimis Temporibus, 30 November 1967 part I, #4.

[45] Vatican II, Lumen Gentium #10.

46 SCC, Directory #6

47 Synod of Bishops, Ultimis Temporibus, Part I # 5.

48 SCC, Directory #6

49 SCC, Directory #2

50 Ibid. #2.

51 Ibid. #3 and #4.

52 Pope John Paul II, Novo *Incipiente Nostro* (Letter to Priests, 1979) #4.

53 Pope Pius XII, encyclical, Mediator Dei, 1947, #44.

54 Pope Pius XII, *Mediator Dei,* #45,; see also Catechism of the Catholic Church, promulgated by Pope John Paul II, 1994, #1539, #1544, #548.

55 St. Alphonsus De Liguori, *Dignity and Duties of the Priest,* ed. Rev. Eugene Grimm (Brooklyn: Redemptorist Fathers, 1927) pp. 23 and 24, quotation, p. 24.

56 See Isaiah 6:1-8.

57 See Fulton J. Sheen, *Treasure in Clay,* Doubleday & Company Inc. Garden City, New York, 1980, pp. 32-35.

58 Luke 5:1-11

59 Fulton J. Sheen, op.cit. pp. 329-330.

60 Romans 8:28-30.

61 John 15:5.

62 Hebrews 5:1-3.

63 Fulton J. Sheen, op. Cit. Pp 329-330.

64 The author of this prayer of praise is not known.

65 Culled from the homily of Pope Benedict XVI at the Chrism Mass on Holy Thursday at St. Peter's Basilica, Rome, April 13, 2006.

66 Donald Knox, Retreat For Priests, Sheed and Ward, New York, 1946, p. 113.

67 Cf. Mk 2: and 7-12.

68 John 20:23.

69 St. Alphonsus Liguori, *The Dignity and Duties of the Priest,* p. 28.

70 St. John Vianney, *The Little Catechism of the Cure of Ars* (Rockford, Illinois: Tan Books and Publishing Inc., 1951), p. 34.

71 Ibid. p.36.

72   Pope John Paul II, Novo Incipiente Nostro (Letter to Priests 1979) #10.

73   St. John Vianney, op. cit. p. 35.

74   Ex. 19:5; 24:7-8.

75   Ex. 24:3-8.

76   Mt. 26:28; Mk. 14:24; Lk. 22:20; 1 Cor 11:25.

77   Cf. Jer 31:31-34; Ezk. 36:25-26; Hos 2:20 ff.

78   A symbolic action is an action performed to stand for an event that is imminent and irrevocable. See, for instance, Ezekiel 12:1-18. Jesus' Last Supper was a symbolic action of his imminent and irrevocable death. Fr. Kieran C. Okoro, Interreligious Dialogue after Vatican II and the Universal Significance of Jesus, (Owerri: Assumpta Press, 2000), P. 75.

79   Vatican II: *Constitution on the Church or Lumen Gentium* (hereinafter LG) #3; see also Pope John Paul II, Ecclesia de Eucharistia (Rome 2003) 21.

80   St. John Vianney, op. cit. pp. 35 and 36.

81   John 15:14.

82   John 15:4-5.

83   Vatican II, *The Ministry and Life of Priests (Presbytorum Ordinis, hereinafter, P. O.)* #12.

84   See John 15:15.

85   Thomas Akempis, *The Imitation of Christ*, Bk IV ch. 8.

86   Is. 49:1; Jer. 1:5.

87   Ps 118 :23.

88   1Cor 1:27.

89   Ex. 3:11.

90   Judges 6:15

91   1 Sam 16:5-13.

92   Jer 1:6.

93   Ps. 116:12-13.

94   St. Augustine, Sermon 329 in Natali Martyrum: PL. 38, 1454-1456 cited as the second reading in the Office of Reading, common of one martyr.

[95] See Rose Adaure Njoku, Owerri Diocese, P. 37.

[96] Ibid. Pp. 30 and 31.

[97] 2Tim 4:6-8.

[98] Vatican II, *Presbyterorum Ordinis*, (hereinafter P.O.)—on the Ministry and Life of Priests # 5.

[99] John P. Schanz, *The Sacraments of Life and Worship* (Milwaukee: The Bruce Publishing Co., 1966), pp. 147-148.

[100] Bernard Cooke, *The Eucharist: Mystery of Friendship*, (Ohio: Geo A. Pflaum Publisher, 1969) pp. 114-115.

[101] Cf. Denzinger and Schonmetzer (hereinafter DS) eds., #1752.

[102] Pope John Paul II, *Dominicae Caenae (1980)* #2; see also Vatican II, *Lumen Gentium* #28; P.O. #2.

[103] Pope John Paul II, *Domincae Caenae: On the Mystery and Worship of the Eucharist* (February 24, 1980) #2.

[104] Pope John Paul II, *Ecclesia de Eucharistia*—Encyclical Letter, (April 17, 2003) #28.

[105] Pope John Paul II, ibid. #29.

[106] Vatican II, P.O. # 6; cf. John Paul II, *Ecclesia de Eucharistia* # 33

[107] Vatican II, P.O. #13; Pope John Paul II, *Ecclesia de Eucharistia* # 31; cf. Code of Canon Law: canon # 904.

[108] Pope John Paul II, Dominicae *Caenae* # 12.

[109] Ibid. #12

[110] Pope Benedict XVI 's homily at the ordination of new priests for the diocese
of Rome on April 29, 2007.

[111] SCC, Directory, #48; cf. Vatican II, P.O. #5.

[112] Pope John Paul II, *Ecclesia de Eucharistia* # 31 and #32.

[113] Cf. Philippians 2:5.

[114] Philippians 4:13.

[115] By the fact of his intending to celebrate and actually celebrating the Mass as a competent minister of the Catholic Church, that Mass is automatically valid. This is the meaning of the Latin phrase *ex opere operato*.

[116] Cf. SCC, *Directory* #48 and 49.

117 Cf. John 6:56.

118 *The Rites of the Catholic Church as revised by the Second Vatican Ecumenical Council vol II* (New York: Pueblo Publishing Co.) p. 84.

119 Fr. M. Eugene Boylan, *The Spiritual Life of the Priest* (Westminster, Maryland: Newman Press, 1953) pp. 53-57.

120 Pope John Paul II, Apostolic Letter *Mane Nobiscum Domine* 2004, #24.

121 Ibid. #25.

122 Cf. ibid. #26.

123 Fulton J. Sheen, *Treasure in Clay*, p. 188.

124 Francis Trochu, *The Cure D'Ars: St. Jean Marie Baptiste Vianney* (Westminster, Maryland: The Newman Press, 1949), pp. 116-117.

125 Ibid 257-338.

126 Ibid. pp. 305-307.

127 Pope John Paul II, *Mane Nobiscum Domine* #30.

128 Ibid. #18.

129 See Exodus 34:27-35.

130 SCC, *Directory #50*.

131 1 Thessalonians 4:3-8.

132 1 Corinthians (hereinafter 1 Cor.) 6:9-20.

133 1 Cor. 3:17.

129 See Raniero Cantalmessa, "Glorify God in Your Bodies: Our Call To Horizontal Holiness" in *"Be Holy!" : God's First Call To Priests Today [The Talks From the Worldwide Retreat For Priests]* ed. By Fr. Tom Forrest, (South Bend, Indiana: Greenlawn Press, 1984), pp.18ff.

135 Gerald Kelly, *Modern Youth and Chastity*, (Liguori, Missouri: Liguorian Queen's Work Pamphlets, 1964), p.56

136 Gerald Kelly, *Modern Youth and Chastity*, p. 14.

137 Ibid. p. 14.

138 Ibid. p. 27.

139 Ibid. pp.19 and 20.

140 Ibid. pp. 20 and 21.

141 God's purpose for giving this type of natural attraction is to lead the persons to marry. For it locks the hearts of the two together to the

exclusion of others. Hence, it is an aid to fidelity, stability, and happiness in marriage. It is therefore a good thing to have before marriage and a very necessary thing to cultivate in marriage. But those who are married must bear mind that this type of attraction is emotion, and like other emotions, it is not permanent. It needs to be cultivated by a conscious endeavour to preserve those qualities that were present at the beginning of marriage, to be always conscious of those things that bring joy to the other party. And since this attraction is blind, those choosing marriage partners must be humble enough to listen to the advice of relatives and friends. See Gerald Kelly, op. cit. pp.22 and 23.

[142] Ibid. pp.24-25.

[143] Ibid. p. 8.

[144] Ibid. pp. 10 and 11.

[145] Ibid. pp. 11 and 12.

[146] Ibid. p. 13.

[147] Judith 10-13.

[148] Fulton J. Sheen, *Treasure in Clay* (Garden City, New York: Doubleday & Co., Inc., 1980) p. 204.

[149] Genesis 1:27-28; 2:18-24.

[150] Mark 10:1-12; Mt. 19:1-9.

[151] Jn. 2:1-11.

[152] See Pope Pius XI, *Casti Cannubi* (13 December 1930) #1 and #38.

[153] Synod of Bishops (1967) *Ultimis Temporibus* part II #4.

[154] Vatican II, *Decree on the Ministry and Life of Priests* (hereinafter, *P. O.*) #16.

[155] Lk. 18:29-30.

[156] Mt. 19:10-12.

[157] Acts 5:1-10

[158] 1 Cor. 7:32-33. See also Vatican II, *P.O.* #16.

[159] See Fulton J Sheen, *Treasure in Clay* p. 206.

[160] Mt. 22:30ff; cf. also Mark 12:25.

[161] Genesis 3:15, and Revelations 12:1-17

[162] Pope John Paul II, *Letter to Priests for Holy Thursday 1988, #1* and #2; Eugene Boylan, *The Spiritual Life of the Priest* (Westminster, Maryland: The Newman Press, 1953), pp. 139-140.

[163] Vatican II, *Dogmatic Constitution on the Church* (hereinafter *Lumen Gentium or simply LG*) # 58; cf. Pope John Paul II, *Letter to Priests on Holy Thursday 1988* #2.

[164] *God Alone: The Collected Writings of St. Louis Mary de Montfort [hereinafter De Montfort, God Alone]* (Bay Shore, New York : Montfort Publications, 1987), p. 294.

[165] Luke 1:35.

[166] Quoted in De Montfort, *God Alone,* p. 294.

[167] Ibid. pp. 294-295.

[168] Ibid. pp295-296.

[169] Ibid. pp.296-297.

[170] Luke 1:39-55. The *Magnificat* is also part of the prayers of the Legion of Mary, where it is called *The Catena Legionis* (or *The Legion's Chain*). See Concilium Legionis Mariae, *The Official Handbook of the Legion of Mary* (Dublin, Ireland: De Montfort House), December 1993, pp. 132-133.

[171] Frederick William Faber, *The Foot of the Cross* (hereinafter, Faber, *The Foot of the Cross),* new ed. (Rockford, Illinois: Tan Books and Publishers, Inc., 1956 and 1978) p. 81.

[172] Ibid. pp.96-99.

[173] Ibid. p. 104.

[174] Ibid. 108.

[175] Ibid. p. 109.

[176] Ibid. pp.115-116.

[177] Fulton Sheen, *Treasure in Clay,* pp. 117-118.

[178] Faber, *The Foot of the Cross* p, 116.

[179] Ibid. pp. 130-131.

[180] Ibid. pp. 143-144. See also 1 Corinthians 13:1-13.

[181] Faber, *The Foot of the Cross,* p.144.

[182] Ibid. pp. 145 and 146.

[183] Ibid. p. 148.

[184] Faber, op. cit. p.183.

[185] Federico Suarez, *About Being a Priest* (Houston: Lumen Christi Press, 1979), pp. 211 and 212.

[186] Suarez, Ibid. p. 212.

[187] Pope John Paul II, *Rosarium Virginis Mariae* 2002, #3.

[188] See FR. Luis Kondor, ed. *Fatima in Lucia's Own Words* (Postulation Centre, Fatima, Portugal, 1976), p. 28 and passim; also *Dictionary of Saints,* s.v. "Mary"; s.v. "Soubirous, Marie Bernarde."

[189] De Montfort, *God Alone,* p.152.

[190] See *Divine Office* vol. III (London-Glasgow, 1974), p. 319*; De Montfort, *God Alone,* p. 217.

[191] Pope John Paul, *Rosarium Virginis Mariae,* October 2002, #1 and 2

[192] Pope John Paul II, *Rosarium Virginis Mariae* #18.

[193] This was the suggestion of Pope John II see FOOD FOR THE POOR INC. (Deer field Beach, Florida), A New Guide to Praying the Rosary.

[194] Suarez, *About Being a Priest* p. 213.

[195] Paul A. Fisher, *Behind the Lodge Door* (Rockford: Tan Books and Publishers, Inc., 1944, p. 25.

[196] *The Permanent Instruction of the Alta Vendita: A Masonic Blueprint for the Subversion of the Catholic Church.* Edited by John Vennari (Rockford, Illinois: Tan Books and Publishers Inc.) 1999, pp.1 and 2.

[197] Ibid. pp.2 and 3; see also Paul A. Fisher, *Behind the Lodge Door* (Rockford: Tan Books and Publishers, Inc., 1994), p.39.

[198] John Vennari, op. cit. p. 5.

[199] Ibid. pp.8-10.

[200] Pope Leo XIII, Humanum Genus (1884) #2; see also Charles Madden, *Freemasonry, Mankind's Hidden Enemy* (Rockford, Illinois: Tan Books and Publishers, Inc., 2005), p. 6

[201] Pope Leo XIII, op. cit. #10.

[202] Pope Leo XIII, *Humanum Genus* #16.

[203] John Vennari, op. cit. pp.11-13.

[204] Ibid. p.14.

[205] Michael Rose, *Goodbye, Good men: How Liberals Brought Corruption into the Catholic Church* (Washington DC: Regnery Publishing, Inc., 2002) pp.2 and 3.

[206] Ibid. pp. 3 and 4.

[207] Ibid. P. 9.

[208] Ibid. pp. 9 and 10.

[209] Ibid. P.45.

[210] Ibid. pp 10 and 11.

[211] See Rose, ibid. p. 15.

[212] Ibid. p.28

[213] Ibid. pp. 28-30. quotation p. 30.

[214] Rose, ibid. pp. 34 and 35.

[215] Ibid. p. 36.

[216] See Rose, ibid. p. 56.

[217] See "St. John's Seminary Leaders Failing The Catholic Church" *The Wanderer* 4 July2002, p.1; also "Begone Satan," p. 6.

[218] "Real Men Don't Become Priests," *The Catholic World Report* (San Francisco) July 2002, p. 23.

[219] Rose, op. cit. pp. 56-58.

[220] Ibid. pp.59-61.

[221] Ibid. pp. 60, 65-69.

[222] Ibid. pp. 60, 77-85.

[223] Ibid. p.90

[224] Ibid. pp. 95-97.

[225] C.f. *National Catholic Register* (Denver)June 30-6 July 2002, p.10.,

[226] Rose, op. cit. pp. 100-107.

[227] See Pope Leo XIII, Humanum Genus #20.

[228] Rose, pp.89-92.

[229] Ibid. p.94.

[230] Ibid. p. 98.

[231] Cf. ibid. p. 100.

[232] Ibid. p. 108.

[233] Ibid. pp. 111-112.

[234] There is clearly here the hand of Freemasons, whose first step is usually to lower the faith and moral of the people who will then fall victim to their plan. See Pope Leo XIII, op. cit. #20

[235] Rose, op. cit. pp. 115-116.

[236] Ibid. pp. 126-127.

[237] See Rose, ibid. p. 119.

[238] Ibid. P. 118.

[239] Ibid. pp. 118-119.

[240] Ibid. pp123 and 124.

[241] Ibid. P. 130.

[242] Ibid. p. 131.

[243] Ibid. p. 132.

[244] Ibid. pp.142-143; see also pp. 39-40.

[245] See Rose, *Goodbye, Good men, pp. 194-195.*

[246] Paul Likoudis, AMCHURCH COMES OUT(hereinafter *Amchurch Comes Out*): *The U. S. Bishops, Pedophile Scandals and the Homosexual Agenda* (Petersburg, Illinois: Roman Catholic Faithful, Inc., 2002), p.136.

[247] Likoudis, ibid. pp.137,140-141.

[248] Paul A. Fisher, *Behind the Lodge Door,* pp. 192-199.

[249] Ibid. p. 200.

[250] Congregation for the Doctrine of the Faith, "Declaration on Masonic Associations" November 26, 1983. This document was signed by Cardinal Joseph Ratzinger and Archbishop Jerome Hamer, prefect and secretary respectively. See also Paul Fisher, op. cit. p. 201.

[251] This movement is most likely a work or part of the Freemasonry, which glories in concealment of its name often in dangerous undertakings. See Paul A. Fisher, *Behind the Lodge Door* pp. 29 and30.

[252] Rose, Goodbye, Good Men, pp. 198-199.

[253] See Paul A. Fisher, op. cit. p. 29

[254] Rose, op. cit. p. 200.

[255] Ibid. pp. 199-201.

[256] Rose, Op. cit. p. 206

[257] Pope Pius XI, *Divini Illius Magistri* 1929, #78.

[258] Rose, op.cit. p. 206.

[259] Rose, Goodbye, Good Men, p. 210; also "Albany Bishop Launches New Initiative For Lay—Run Church," *Wanderer* (St. Paul Min.) 13 July 2006, p. 1.

[260] "Pontiff Sees Need for Recovery of Eucharist," *Zenith* 11 May 2006, p. 1.

[261] See Michael Rose, op. cit. p. 35.

[262] See "Begone, Satan!" *The Wanderer* (St. Paul, Minnesota) 11 July 2002, p. 6.

[263] Ibid.

[264] "Pope: Abuse a source of shame" *The Bulletin* (Bend, Oregon) 29 July 2002, pp. 1and 4.

[265] See "It Isn't Just Sex Abuse" *The Wanderer* (*National Catholic Weekly*), 4 July 2002, p. 9

[266] Vatican II, *Optatam Totius* #5; John Paul II, *Pastores Dabo Vobis* w#60-62.

[267] This was done by Bishop Robert Vasa of the Diocese of Baker, Oregon.

[268] See 1 Tim. 2:4.

[269] Vincent P. Miceli, *THE GODS OF ATHEISM* (Harrison, New York: Roman Catholic Books, 1971), p. 446

[270] See Luke 23:31; 22:12-19.

[271] "Redemption Comes Through The Jews . . . Jewish Businessman, Sam Miller, Wraps Anti-Catholic Bias in News Media." Buckeye Bulletin (Cleveland Diocese) May-June, 2010.